CASUALTY

THE INSIDE STORY

Hilary Kingsley

BBC BOOKS

For Hatty, Anna and Daniel

ACKNOWLEDGEMENTS

This book was a pleasure to research and write because the people in the *Casualty* team are normal, helpful and interesting. I suspect they are immunised in some way before being allowed into the Bristol warehouse where the shows are made. At any rate, self-esteem, problems and 'luvvie' tendencies aren't apparent. Perhaps they could pass on the secret to colleagues elsewhere in television.

I would particularly like to thank Geraint Morris without whom *Casualty* would never have become the important series it is. I am also grateful to Shaun Lee Houghton and the other members of The Casualty Fan Club (PO Box 535, Burslem, Stoke-on-Trent, Staffordshire ST6 2PH).

PICTURE CREDITS

British Film Institute 11 (top); Nigel Parry/Katz Pictures colour page 4; Turner Entertainment 11 (lower right). *Courtesy acknowledgements:* Jeremy Brock and Paul Unwin 6; Ginnie Hole 101; Geraint Morris 8; Peter Salt 9, 81; The Richard Stone Partnership 25; Simon Tytherleigh 72–75, 78, 87, 122, colour page 2. All other pictures © BBC.

With special thanks to Patricia Taylor and Simon Tytherleigh.

This book is published to accompany the
television series entitled *Casualty*.
Published by BBC Books,
a division of BBC Enterprises Limited,
Woodlands, 80 Wood Lane, London W12 0TT

First published 1993
© Hilary Kingsley 1993
ISBN 0 563 36936 1
Designed by Roger Daniels
Typeset by Goodfellow & Egan Ltd, Cambridge
Printed and bound in Great Britain by
Richard Clays Ltd, St Ives Plc
Colour separation by Technik Ltd, Berkhampsted
Cover printed by Richard Clays Ltd, St Ives Plc

CONTENTS

FIRST TWINGES

6

HISTORY IN THE MAKING

14

WHO'S WHO IN HOLBY

44

OPERATION HIT DRAMA

72

HICCUPS

92

CASENOTES

102

THE TROLLEYS ROLL FOR 1993

124

Above the din of voices, footsteps, clanking trolleys and ringing telephones came a sound like a dog howling in the distance. A distraught father moaned, 'Not Tony, not my son! Oh God, not my son!'

In a sideroom in the accident and emergency department of Bristol Royal Infirmary, a male charge nurse was calmly but clearly telling the man and his wife that their teenage son had been killed in a road crash.

On the other side of the venetian blind, trying not to listen, were Jeremy Brock and Paul Unwin, friends from the time they had put on a play together at Bristol University, now would-be creators of a television series. They were trying to think about everything that the nurse, Peter Salt, had talked them through in the hour before one of his colleagues had approached and nodded at the couple arriving and he'd politely excused himself.

Before they knew it, Peter had handed the parents over to another nurse and was back, relaxed, concentrating on the boys from the BBC, asking what they'd like to see next.

Jeremy Brock recalls, 'We were stunned. We couldn't miss these terrible sounds and we were moved. Yet there he was – chatting to us as before. He'd been five minutes, just as he said he'd be.

'There was no question of cynicism, he had been sincere with those poor people. He knew he was witnessing the worst moment of their lives. But he had switched gear almost instantly. We suddenly saw that he had to do it, that all the staff there had to do it, otherwise they simply couldn't function. They were put in positions of extraordinary stress, yet they had to deal with things as though they were ordinary. Most of us would take years to get over the situations they deal with every day.'

From the pain of those parents, *Casualty* was

FIRST TWINGES

In 1984 two bright sparks, Paul Unwin (left) and Jeremy Brock (right) had an idea for a television show. It stayed in a drawer until a cry was heard in a BBC corridor – 'hospital drama – quick'.

born. 'We'd had this vague idea about an accident and emergency ward for the television series and we'd sketched in a group of characters. But it wasn't until that moment that we both knew we were right. We knew we were dealing with heroes and that we had to focus on nurses like Peter. Most of all, we had to be truthful.'

In 1984 the problem shared by Jeremy Brock and Paul Unwin wasn't medical. They were, they now remember, both entirely healthy but 'desperately broke'. In their mid-twenties, with interesting but low-paid jobs (Jeremy was about to start as a trainee script editor at the BBC, Paul was directing plays at the Bristol Old Vic), they were sitting round the table in Paul's kitchen in Hackney, London, when they hit on the answer. They'd dream up a telly series and the money would roll in. Yeah!

The sort of series this should be evolved over the next few hours as they worked through the list of TV shows they liked and disliked.

'I think we started with *Angels*, which had been fairly successful in its way. We found we both loved *M.A.S.H.* and *Hill Street Blues*, shows where there were several stories being told at once and where the characters were slightly bigger than life,' says Brock.

'We kept coming back to the idea of a hospital, perhaps because we're both neurotic and hypochondriacs. Paul had been in hospital after a car smash and I'd been in with a gut complaint. We began swapping anecdotes. I remembered there'd been a sign in my hospital, "Beware Falling Masonry", and we agreed it was crazy.'

Unwin adds, wryly, 'We began to take it very, very seriously because there was a lot of concern about the running down of the National Health Service then. We wanted to do a campaigning programme with that feeling of being on the ground, in the thick of it.

'We wrote it down on a couple of pages and called it *Front Line*. We weren't hindered by knowledge. That was the great thing about being green. You could get that excited!' That couple of pages, like so many bearing such world-stopping ideas, went nowhere for a year.

By 1985 Brock was script editor on the Saturday night police series *Juliet Bravo*. The pro-

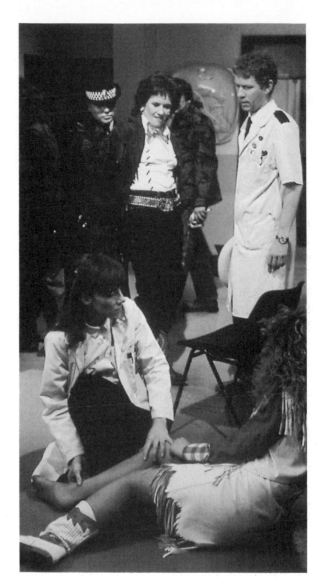

Accident and Emergency – the bad behaviour ward

ducer was a humorous, enthusiastic Welshman, Geraint Morris, respected within the BBC for his work on *Softly Softly*, *The Onedin Line* and *Juliet Bravo*. His associate producer was Michael Bartley. Morris and Bartley were to tell their young colleague about a request from the then Controller of BBC1, Michael Grade, for outlines for a hospital drama series. Copies to the head of the drama department, Jonathan Powell. Fast.

Brock dusted off the Hackney blueprint for *Front Line* which began, he smiles to recall, with the proclamation: 'In 1945 a dream was born in the National Health Service. In 1985 that dream is in tatters.'

It had gone on to sketch out Charlie, a charge nurse, Megan, a motherly female nurse, Kuba, a Polish porter, and Clive, a nurse with a drink problem. They'd done no research because they didn't know how to go about it.

Jonathan Powell read the two pages and told them to flesh them out with a complete treatment. They poured out their passion. He said, 'Write me one episode and outlines for twelve more.'

By then Brock was working hard on *Juliet Bravo* scripts. Unwin was directing a pantomime for the theatre by day, reading up on 'blood and guts' for TV at night. On days off, with Morris' help, the pair began loitering in the A & E department of the Bristol Royal Infirmary. That's when the hard work began.

They didn't know it but Charlie, Megan, Kuba and co. were in a race with Hannah Gordon and her staff at a fictional cottage hospital in the Lake District. Almost any series featuring pretty, petite Hannah, a leading television star from such 1970s comedies as *My Wife Next Door* and such drama serials as *Upstairs Downstairs* and *Telford's Change*, would have had a high chance of success at that time. And cottage hospitals were perceived as places of character and caring.

Geraint Morris, *Casualty*'s long-serving producer

Yet, despite the romantic possibilities — a succession of male patients falling for the wonderful woman in a white coat — the colourful scenery, and the relative safety of the idea, Powell plumped for the grey and gritty setting of a large, inner city hospital. As it turned out the writing had been on the walls of cottage hospitals. They're now almost extinct within the NHS.

Instead, the plans for Holby City were approved. It would be staffed by unglamorous people with untidy lives. Into it would flock the careless, the careworn, the drunk, the addicted, the crushed, the bashed, the mad and the bad. It would not be a place of quiet sanctuary and respect. It would be an extension of the street, a rough street at that, in which medical miracles were rare and damage limitation was often the best that could be achieved. Its stories and style would upset politicians, irritate health workers and open wounds in the minds of some of its audience.

Brock, Unwin and Morris were delighted. They were never to grow rich from it and critical acclaim was slow in coming. But they were launching the show that was to become the BBC's most important and successful fifty-minute drama. Other medical dramas were to seem anaemic by comparison.

Peter Salt's life was to change. His work of caring for patients and running a busy department at the BRI would take on another dimension. Over the next eight years his experiences and judgements would feed ideas to a succession of writers, most of them as green and medically illiterate as Brock and Unwin had been. His expertise would correct a succession of actors' mistakes. In a sense, his reception area was to be packed, eventually, with around 16 million attentive armchair patients.

A Suitable Case for Television Treatment

I have a friend who claims he would need an anaesthetic to watch an episode of *Casualty*. 'Don't you find it depressing? How can you enjoy that catalogue of miseries, the tumbling entrails, the fake bodies shuddering under the electric shocks? You sick or something?' he asks.

It sounds lame, I suppose, to say that an interest in illness and unhappiness is completely healthy. *Casualty's* popularity is certainly no accident. It works because there's

Peter Salt, the nurse who impressed

a skilful blending of two fictional streams, the medical drama and the soap opera, and two documentary streams, the how-surgery-is-done scientific programme and the political report which highlights cock-ups and cut-backs and points the finger of blame.

Back in the 1950s the fictional and factual strands were miles apart. Television's view of hospitals had been confined to the soppy soapy tales in *Emergency! Ward 10*, the twice-weekly serial where no worryingly incurable illnesses were ever contracted, the annual death rate was five, later reduced to two, and the only really gory sight was a nurse's too-vivid lipstick.

The BBC's *Your Life in their Hands*, which took cameras into real operating theatres to show real throbbing innards, ran for six years from 1958

regularly attracting audiences of 10 million and regularly upsetting the British Medical Association. Doctors said it was 'pandering to the morbid' and seemed to fear that patients might no longer take their orders lying down.

But despite the claims that such documentaries caused shocks (there were early reports of panic accidents and suicides by people fearing they too had the symptoms or needed the surgery they'd seen), the overriding response to seeing surgeons at work was, 'Well, I never! Isn't that clever?' I doubt many of us actually understood that much more about anatomy or the development of disease but we found our stomachs were stronger than we'd thought.

Over the next two decades television studied organ transplants, pregnancy and childbirth, treatments for infertility and for most of the major diseases. Series such as *World in Action* also took the nation's pulse, memorably over tuberculosis, and urged checks and reforms. Telegenic doctors like Miriam Stoppard learned to hold microphones and read autocues and in *Where There's Life* encouraged 'ordinary' people to talk about their bodies.

Fewer and fewer viewers fainted. Not even when a breathless presenter on 1992's *Hospital Watch* produced a warm tumour fresh from a woman's womb and sliced it up before our very eyes. Not even when a Japanese surgeon in BBC2's *The Trouble with Medicine* showed the anxious relatives of a cancer patient being wheeled from the operating theatre the whole pink breast he'd had to remove.

Our 'bravery' was due partly to the medical qualifications we had been gaining from television drama. Book publishers had long ago spotted that anything to do with 'angels of mercy', doctors and nurses, chronicling triumphs over tragedy, sold well. The fascination went back at least as far as the 1920s to the doctor tales of Somerset Maugham and, later, AJ Cronin who invented Dr Finlay, his Casebook, wee Janet and all. (Such an interest in medical matters probably didn't exist before this century. The doctor with his leeches and potions wasn't that much use.)

Doctor and nurse romance was a strong early strand in the Mills and Boon market. Richard Gordon added humour with his *Doctor in the House* books. *Sue Barton, Student Nurse*, inspired generations of schoolgirls.

Why the fascination exists is obvious. Surgeries, clinics and hospitals deal in life and death and we have a vested interest. We all want to stay alive, we don't want to die. Maybe we can pick up the odd survival tip by reading the novel or watching the show. And we all visit doctors from time to time. Doctors rely on, and used to rely much more on, a kind of remoteness, almost a kind of godhead. They have the knowledge and we don't. 'Doctor knows best' is a phrase passed on by everybody's mother. Ours not to reason why, ours just to take the pills.

Reading about doctors, or seeing them on screen, as people with everyday problems and feelings dissolves that mystique. We like that. At the same time we still need to believe in the doctor's special powers, the touch of magic, that will fix the griping tummy, the aching leg, the

'Doctor knows best' is a phrase passed on by everybody's mother. Ours not to reason why, ours just to take the pills.

infected wound and keep us alive. A small dose of medical jargon usually does the trick.

The 1950s heroes came from *Ward 10*, and moist-eyed Dr Kildare's idealistic life and times at Blair Hospital made actor Richard Chamberlain the cleanest pin-up of the 1960s and a BBC star. His hairy-armed rival Vince Edwards as Ben Casey in another American dishy doc show was meanwhile soothing viewers of ITV.

During the 1970s America gave us the wicked humour and sexiness of *M.A.S.H.*, life in the 4077th Mobile Army Surgical Hospital during the war in Korea (for which read Vietnam). It seemed to inhibit British drama scriptwriters who could manage nothing more addictive than *General Hospital*, a similar prescription to *Emergency! Ward 10*.

GF Newman's damning four-part saga *The Nation's Health* in 1983, suggesting that the whole health service was diseased, class-ridden and doomed, may have helped to cancel plans for cosier series.

But by then Steven Bochco's *St Elsewhere*, featuring a run-down Boston hospital staffed by mainly young, confused, wise-cracking medics struggling to make sense of a violent, soul-less world, was changing hospital drama for ever. Surgery could no longer be performed to a background of soaring strings and ending with relatives' happy tears.

The style of soap opera had also been changing, even if its basic ingredients − intertwined unending stories about a group of people, living or working as a family and depending on each other − had not. Decorative young docs swinging their stethoscopes and coquettish nurses

Often something missing in those old medical shows – *Emergency! Ward 10* (right), *Angels* (below) and *Dr Kildare* (below, right) – like patients, blood, realism

waggling syringes may still have a place in the daytime soaps of America and Australia. But *The Young Doctors* and even Germany's hugely-loved *Black Forest Clinic* were jokes in Britain as *EastEnders* set the fashion for tough talk and life in the raw.

The appeal of soap, or continuing drama as its producers sometimes insist on calling it, has never diminished as the ratings league always shows. We watch, dissect and relate to our own lives what's happening to the characters we know so well and for whom, fight as we might, we care.

In *Casualty* the doctors, nurses, paramedics, managers, receptionists and porters of a big city hospital are the soap regulars. Their dramas catch and hold the audiences as the series unfolds. To them are added each week a quota of mini-dramas which are not soapy, because they have beginnings and ends, but deal in the same currency.

Broken relationships, missing children, despair at unemployment, homelessness, drink and drug problems, social, sexual and psychological crises

In episode one Suzie and Kuba guess the gas

figure consistently in *EastEnders* and *Brookside*. They also figure in the confessions that gush faster than blood from victims and relatives who come into Holby after the road crash, the accident at work, in the living room or in the football stadium.

Combining the values of soap, a punchy political concern, documentary reportage and the thrilling elements of fast-action disaster movies, *Casualty* manages to be both chronically comforting and often acutely exciting.

While we understand Charlie, Duffy, Julian and many more as human beings, we also still see them as magical practitioners who talk in an alien tongue. We don't understand when Mike Barratt orders 30cc of atrophine, or says they'll have to defibrilate the upper thorax, but we sense that some technical wizardry is going on and we find that reasssuring. If it ever happens to us, the gang down at our local A & E will weave the same spell.

But of course the true, hidden reason why we love *Casualty* is that it is NOT happening to us. It is happening to someone else. Deeper than the sympathy we feel for Holby's injured patients is a tiny voice within us that says, 'Phew, I'm glad it's him and not me. It's not my foot they're sawing off. It's not me who's addicted to heroin, I didn't get thrown through the windscreen, I'm not a battered wife...'

There's also a relief that we didn't cause the ghastly accident we just saw because, along with our fear of suffering pain we also fear hurting others, particularly those we love. Watching a fictional version of our fears in safety is a way of confronting those fears. Call it a nasty, smug touch of I'm-all-right. But it is a comfort. When Aristotle and those old Greeks talked of drama purging the mind of pity and terror, they were on to something.

So, the answer for my critical friend is that

Smiles from Holby's first heroes, led by decent Doctor Ewart

surgeon bent over and the knife went in and blood came out there was silence suddenly. They were absolutely riveted. I know my work adds to the dramatic impact.'

Lastly, there is a bit of sexism at play here which I hardly dare mention in connection with a show as politically correct as *Casualty*.

The series appeals to a wide class and age range but women viewers outnumber the men. It may be that women take a higher interest in their own (more complicated) bodies and feel that, as child-bearers, their bodies are machines that must be looked after. It's more likely that the head doctor is male and, in Holby's case, the chief nurse, Charlie, is also male.

In all the doctor-nurse romances and in much of the medical fiction, the male doctor is an authority figure and, in almost every case, the female nurse begins by respecting him to the point of fear. Women viewers often feel a frisson at the sight of a dishy doctor that is stronger than the frisson produced by, say, a dishy solicitor. The reason is that the doctor is the only man in the community, apart from a husband or lover, who has the right to touch. In *Casualty* even when the doctor is a woman, Charlie shares the laying-on-of-hands which watching women need. There is a balancing bit of sexism on the male side. Men do fantasize about women in uniform, I'm afraid. It's something to do with the enforced plainness of the garb provoking a salacious curiosity. What can be going on under that girl copper's no-nonsense blue serge jacket? So a nurse's prim high-necked dress or a woman doctor's white coat excites the same interest.

I know a man who fancies Duffy with her hair up in her nurse's kit but not with her hair loose when she's dressed in civvies. You wouldn't guess it to look at him. There are probably millions more men like him out there.

you don't have to be a ghoul to watch *Casualty*'s spouting gore and think it's a bloody good show. Paul Unwin calls it 'positive voyeurism' and thinks it's a way for us to rehearse our reactions to tragedies which may occur in the future to us or to people we love.

Simon Tytherleigh, who has worked as a make-up artist and prosthetics maker on more episodes of *Casualty* than anyone else, is offended when people accuse him of creating horror for horror's sake.

'When we filmed an episode where a girl's neck was crushed in a football accident and she needed an emergency tracheotomy, I happened to join the other actors and crew as they were lolling around, drinking tea and chatting. They could see the scenes on the monitors and as the

'It was a bit of a bloody mess and it went on being a bit of a bloody mess.' That's how Jonathan Powell recalls Casualty at the start. It was 1985. He was the BBC's Head of Drama Series. Granada had screened their stylish, award-winning serial Jewel in the Crown. But the BBC's only jewel, as too many people had publicly pointed out, had been the American mini-series The Thorn Birds, featuring Dr Kildare in a cassock. Spirits at Television Centre were low. Brock and Unwin's efforts struck absolutely no one as a cause for celebration, or a sign that the BBC's knack of finding the solid, truthful drama series people wanted to follow had not gone for good.

Jonathan Powell recalls, 'Our Saturday night police series, Juliet Bravo, was coming to an end because the leading actress wanted to leave. We had these two ideas for hospital series – the cottage hospital one which was very nice, safe, a Juliet Bravo with a stethoscope show, and this off-the-wall one which posed so many problems. It didn't suit the studio; the fact that a casualty ward is really like a train station – so many people pass through it you can't develop the stories well – seemed limiting and could be repetitive; I wasn't sure the subjects were right for an eight o'clock Saturday slot; it was set at night which made it expensive and difficult to do. Anyway, I discussed it with Michael Grade, who was the Controller, and he said "You decide".

'I went for Casualty because there was a feeling of life and passion in it and, well, I was anxious for new, young people to create something. I put them with a very experienced producer, Geraint Morris, and I hoped for the best.'

In the late summer of 1986 actor Bernard Gallagher appeared on a number of talk shows to discuss his role as Ewart Plimmer, the father of Holby Hospital's accident and emergency

HISTORY IN THE MAKING

At the start, the BBC's hospital drama was described as 'Juliet Bravo with spots and bloody cuts'. It soon caused temperatures to rise and rashes to break out among some who watched it. It wasn't expected to survive. But audiences rallied, Casualty thrived. Then in 1993 its hard-hitting scenes of inner city riots put it on the critical list again.

ward in this new drama series called Casualty. Nothing too surprising there, most viewers must have thought. From 6 September, the beginning of its first run, they knew better.

The first episode, 'Gas', started with Charlie driving to work in his old yellow Beetle car, 'Lover Boy' blaring meaningfully from the radio. (Derek Thompson, the actor who plays him,

Gloves and white coat were off for Holby's first consultant, Ewart Plimmer (Bernard Gallagher)

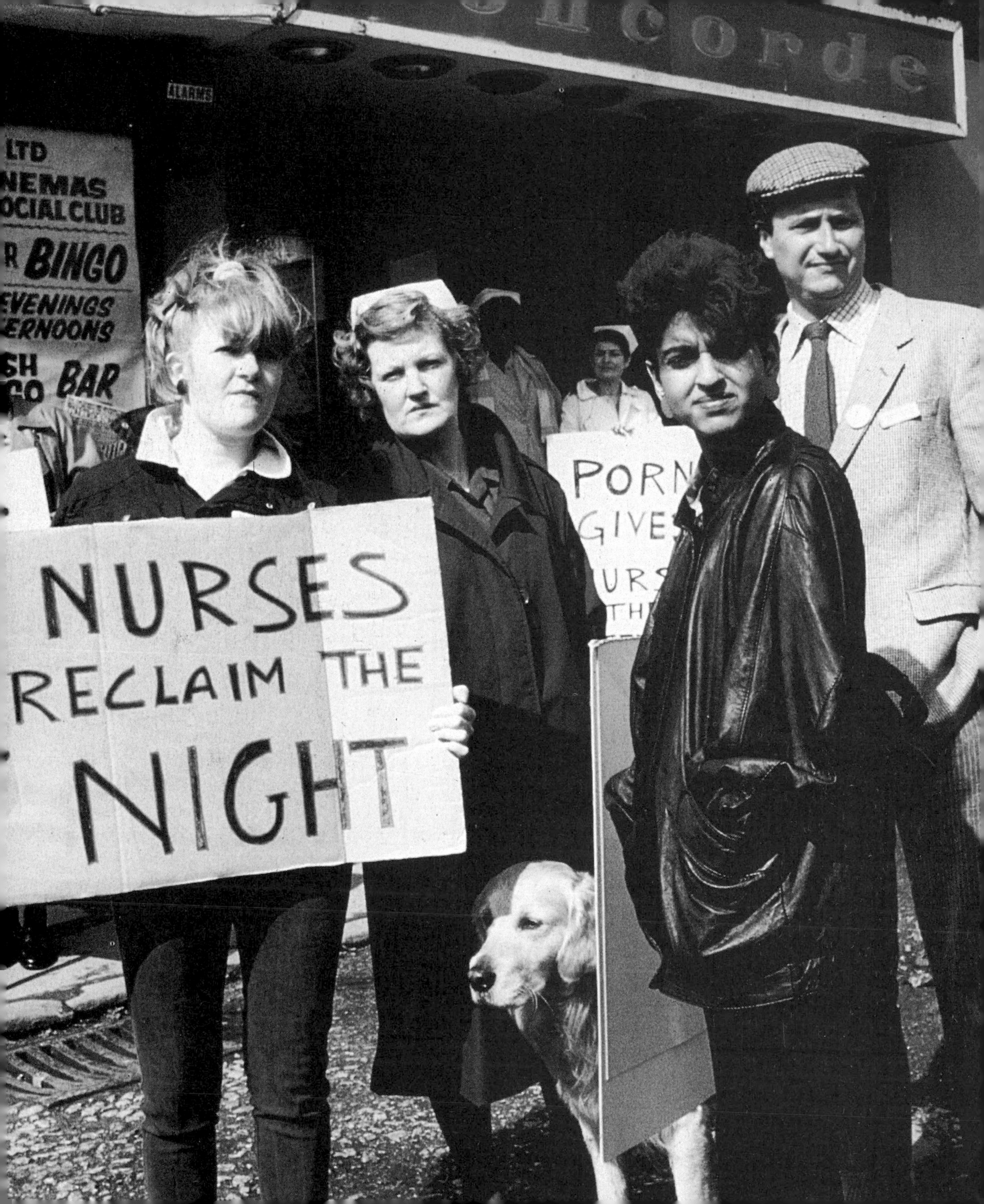
NURSES RECLAIM THE NIGHT
PORN GIVES
LTD
BINGO
EVENINGS
BAR

now jokes: it was 'Noddy goes to hospital'.) He arrived at Holby and stubbed out his fag on the ground with his foot as Ewart Plimmer was heard barking at an ambulance man. When not rowing, Ewart was feet-up at the untidy desk of his poky office, Walkman headphones clamped to his ears. Charlie, Charge Nurse and NUPE rep, was soon yelling, 'Cubicle five needs an enema!' at King, the large, loud male nurse who'd rather have loitered in the staff room, swigging whisky from a bottle in his locker. Meanwhile Baz Samuels, the doctor, was late getting out of bed and arrived breathless and bad tempered. Nurse Duffy, who had a strong Somerset accent, was making fun of colleagues with Susie, the snappy, trendy receptionist. Kuba, the potty Polish porter, was practising a chat-up line and admiring the flowers he'd just pinched from another ward.

The patients were largely unhelpful, unpleasant, drunk or all three. At the end of the shift, Ewart announced, 'A bit of the ceiling fell down in Maternity' and suggested they put up a sign saying 'Beware Falling Masonry' (Jeremy Brock had been determined to get that in, remember.) The final, wry line was Baz's: 'That's what I call preventive medicine!'

As the fourteen other frantically busy episodes went out, it was clear that each of the family of ten regular staff characters led such difficult lives it was a wonder they dragged themselves into work at all. Baz and Charlie were lovers, though she had other friends and after becoming pregnant by accident, underwent an abortion; the ambulance man and his partner were lovers (his wife found out halfway through the series and gave him hell); Ewart's wife had thrown him out, taken him to the cleaners and his daughter had run away; Megan, the saintly SEN, had

No 'naughty nurses' movies here, thank you, protest Duffy (Catherine Shipton) and colleagues

Megan (Brenda Fricker), Holby's best nurse and worst patient

cancer, so she needed a hysterectomy; and fluffy Duffy was attacked on the way to work. We learned later that she was raped. The department was suffering from government spending cuts and was threatened by the prospect of one particularly big cut: the health authority wanted to close it down.

The patients weren't pets, any of them. They included a baby-snatcher, a haemophiliac with a slit wrist refusing treatment because of the Aids panic; a homeless old tramp with shingles; a wife basher and child abuser; an Indian boy who suffered alcohol poisoning; football supporters who stabbed a policeman; junkies attempting suicide; and one of Megan's neighbours who staged a siege in his garden shed, taking a child hostage.

For light relief there was a girl with wind, a boy with his fingers stuck in his bike's handlebars, a macho-man with a boil on his bum and a restaurateur with a missing finger in the strawberry sundae.

There were more than a few 'disgusted of Tunbridge Wells' and elsewhere writing in. By early November Jeremy Brock had had to prepare a four-page explanatory defence document. It should have appeased his superiors, many of whom were suffering post-*Casualty* stress symptoms, had the Tory party but known it. It pointed out that Charlie and Megan smoked but never on duty and stated that more 'don't smoke'

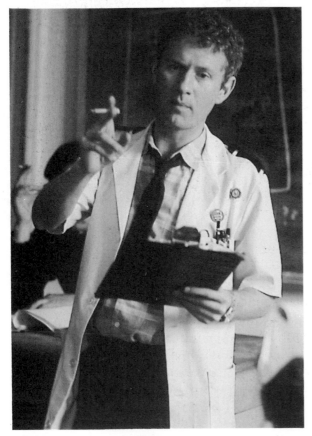

Fuming Charlie Fairhead (Derek Thompson), the nurses' shop steward

comments were being added to future scripts. It pointed out that King joined Alcoholics Anonymous because of his drinking after his friends rallied around. Baz's pill-popping was featured once only and Charlie upbraided her for it, and she and Charlie were seen in bed together only once. It also showed that the political statements were mostly balanced by the opposite points of view.

By this time, a viewer whose address was Rose Cottage, Rose Lane, had written to say he was sending his TV set back after being outraged by the series. The Casualty Surgeons' Association had complained, the Royal College of Nursing had complained. Clwyd North Community Health Council complained that Baz's having more than one lover could encourage the spread of Aids. The Conservative Party Central Office reported that dozens of people had told them that *Casualty* sounded like 'a Labour Party meeting'. The then Junior Health Minister, Edwina Currie, called it inaccurate and criticized it for setting bad examples, particularly in showing staff smoking. The Tory Party Chairman at the time, Norman Tebbitt, added *Casualty* to his BBC programmes' hiss list. Michael Grade reflected at the time: 'In the mood the Tory Party are in at the moment, they would find some political motive in *Bob's Full House.*'

Looking back, Jonathan Powell says, 'The Tebbitt stuff was never that serious. The public were with us. Hospitals *are* run down and underfunded. We thought Mrs Currie may have had a point about the smoking, so we cut down on that in the next series. The row over our drama, *The Monocled Mutineer*, was raging at about the same time and the BBC had shot itself in the foot there by placing newspaper advertising suggesting it was a true story. But with *Casualty*, we had truth on our side.'

Jeremy Brock and Paul Unwin say now that

Boiling Baz (Julia Watson) gives boyfriend Charlie the treatment

they regret upsetting the nurses even if, as they believe, they won them over quickly. 'We went to a conference of A & E nurses at Knutsford and put ourselves up as targets. By the end they saw we were sincere and wanted to tell us stories,' says Paul. They believe the Casualty Surgeons' Association's complaint was absurd but they admit they 'had a ball' getting up politicians' noses.

'What upset the politicians really was that we had characters saying, "The funding of the NHS is not an issue for charity, it's a matter for government responsibility". We showed our regular characters working under ridiculous

pressures for ridiculous money,' Jeremy explains.

Paul Unwin recalls, 'In that first episode, "Gas", we had Kuba the porter discovering what the toxic substance burning the dock workers was after recognizing the distinctive smell of garlic. We had him going into the cubicle on his own and rifling through the notes with Susie the receptionist. That simply wouldn't happen but we thought there was something charming about it. When real hospital staff saw it they went mad.

'We were tub-thumping. But we had to go through that to come out the other side.'

Series Two: Repeating the Prescription

The casual *Casualty* viewer could have been forgiven his or her surprise at discovering that the series had survived for a second run in the autumn of 1987. But long before the politicians had their palpitations over what they saw as a left-wing bias in the first batch of episodes, fifteen new scripts had already been written. What's more, a warehouse on an industrial estate in Bristol had been found and a permanent set built to avoid the costly business of erecting and dismantling Holby in London each week. So, because the money had been spent and many of the shows had been shot, the BBC decided to give them a go – then call it a day.

Accompanying the newspaper publicity stories for the start, on 12 September 1987, was the news that there would be no more programmes. Enough was enough. Geraint Morris was quoted as saying, 'We felt it should end on a high after thirty episodes.' That seemed to be that.

But as Charlie, Duffy, Megan, Ewart and the gang fought to save the night shift, a quieter battle was being waged – and won – behind the scenes. Six weeks on air and Norman Tebbitt had conspicuously not picked up the phone, critics were warming and, following the show's dramatic stabbing involving ambulance girl Sandra Mute, audiences of more than 10 million seemed secure. All these things combined to give the kiss of life to the doomed show. Jonathan Powell's caution disappeared. To writers, cast, crew, medical advisors and make-up designers, the word went out: bleed on.

Perhaps what really saved *Casualty*, strange as it seemed then, was the first 'baddie'. Elizabeth Straker, played by Maureen O'Brien, was a tough but human administrator. She had frequent clashes with the unit's chief, Ewart Plimmer, and was hated so much by him that we just knew

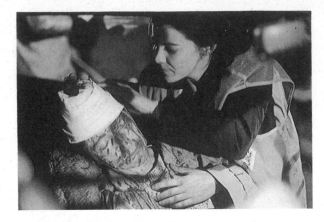

Paramedic Sandra Mute (Lisa Bowerman) tends one of her lucky last patients

they'd eventually have an affair. Which they did. What she also did in the course of the series was to put 'the other side's' point of view. Who said there was no balance?

Mrs Straker was not the only newcomer. Dr Baz had buzzed off (actress Julia Watson hadn't wanted to stay merely as Charlie's girlfriend) and in her place as Casualty Officer at Holby came Mary Tomlinson (Helen Little), an excellent doctor, but no smiler and not one of the gang. There were two new student nurses. One was Karen O'Malley (played by Kate Hardie), a girl who believed in working hard and playing hard. She had an on-off (mostly off) affair with Charlie and provided Duffy with someone to boss about. The second was Cyril James (Eddie Nestor), equally hard-working and ambitious, but when he took decisions on his own, it made Charlie's temperature rise. Like Nurse Martin Ashford, who arrived later, and other black staff, Cyril bore the brunt of racial abuse from patients, particularly those the worse for drink. One charmer even spat at him.

Unit Manager, Elizabeth Straker, has new prescriptions for Ewart

The main thrust of the series was the struggle to save the department. At the start their chances seemed slim. Staff demonstrated on the streets, telling locals that they would have to travel as far as Queen's Hospital, Holby's long-time rival, for emergency treatment if the closure plan went ahead. The regulars managed to have private lives too. Charlie was battling to give up cigarettes between efforts to replace Baz in his life. He saw Karen on a few occasions but she felt he was messing her around. Exasperated, she got herself a job in London. Charlie also applied for a London job but was turned down.

Duffy met Peter Tranter (Eric Deacon), who became her first proper boyfriend since she had been attacked. A well-heeled sports car driving salesman, he offered her an all-expenses-paid trip to California. Duffy said she'd go only if she paid her own way. But a telephone call from Peter's former lover informing him that she was

HIV positive put paid to the plan. He took a test, and was found also to have the Aids virus. He told Duffy, mistakenly believing that as a nurse she would take the news calmly. She was bitterly distressed and eventually confided, not in Megan, but in Dr Mary, a confidence that forged mutual trust between them at last.

Duffy's own test turned out to be negative but meanwhile she had to treat patients who feared they were suffering from Aids. Megan's life was no picnic either. Her husband crashed his cab and was out of work so she had to compensate by working extra hours in a nursing home.

Among others, the gang treated trapped pot holers, victims of an explosion in a block of flats, casualties of a riot in a black community, a meningitis sufferer, a drunk driver, electric shock victims and assorted glue-sniffers, abusive skinheads and drunks.

But undoubtedly the most gripping on-screen

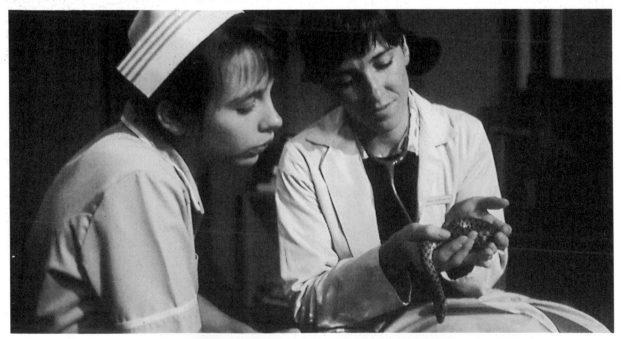

Nurse Karen O'Malley (Kate Hardie) and Dr Mary Tomlinson (Helena Little) share a snake

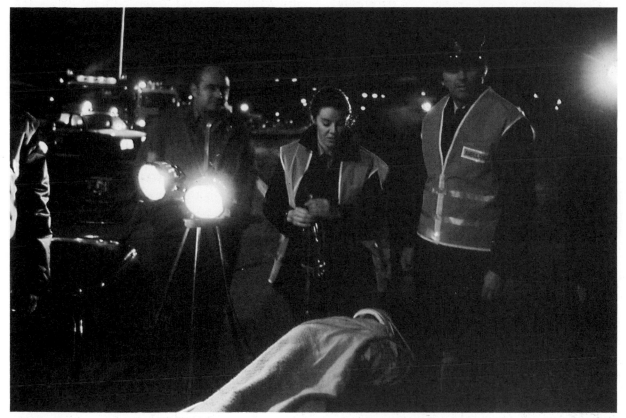

Sandra Mute prepares to meet a stabber and die with excellent ratings

tragedy of the series was the death of pretty dark-haired paramedic Sandra Mute (played by Lisa Bowerman). In episode four she and Andy Ponting, who was by then being divorced by his wife and officially Sandra's fiancé, were called to collect a drunk with a serious head injury. Sandra was treating him in the back of the ambulance when he pulled out a knife and stabbed her in the stomach. He then leapt up and ran off. The team at Holby tried to revive her but Sandra died in crash. Heartbroken, Andy Ponting decided to quit. By episode seven two new paramedics, Jamaican-born Shirley Franklin (Ella Wilder) and Keith Cotterill (Geoffrey Leesley) had taken over.

Off-screen a few weeks later there was an eerie example of life imitating art. On 7 November viewers watched the team helping to dig out the dead and dying from the rubble of a house destroyed by an IRA bomb. Back at Holby poor Irish Megan was blamed by an outraged relative played by Christopher Ellison (best known as DCI Burnside of *The Bill*). Then only hours after the episode was screened an IRA bomb ripped the heart out of Enniskillen. The writers were seen to have put their fingers on the pulse of the nation's current problems without exaggeration. The show may still have been a red rag to some Tory bulls but no one dared call it farfetched again.

Series Three: Keep Taking The Tablets

A new serious-mindedness was descending on Holby's A & E department in the series which began in September 1988, although it wasn't all pain, death and duty. Cyril and Charlie had the chance to play hockey in the corridor at least once.

There were new faces again. Boyish David Rowe (Paul Lacoux) replaced Dr Mary Tomlinson as SHO and Valerie Sinclair (Susan Franklyn) arrived as the Outpatients' Services Manager to do battle with Ewart Plimmer. Elizabeth Straker, we learned, had left to work in America. Although her job was to implement cut-backs, Valerie was humane and caring and there was a mutual attraction when she got to know Charlie. Receptionist Susie had left. In her place was Sadie Tomkins, played by former *Blue Peter* presenter Carole Leader. The new student nurses were Scots lass Alison McGrellis (Julie Graham) and Kiran Joghill (Shaheen Khan), and a medical registrar, played by Brian Capron, appeared frequently, usually to perform a spectacular operation in crash with Dr David.

The patients' problems continued to be serious and painful for some viewers.

A pretty blonde motor mechanic, paralysed from the neck down when a vehicle fell on her, was one chilling cautionary tale. There were

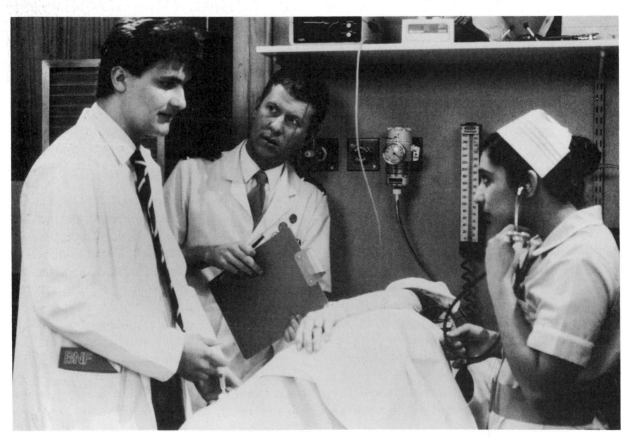

Dr David Rowe (Paul Lacoux) asks student nurse Joghill (Shaheen Khan) what seems to be the trouble

several victims of violence: a security guard who'd been assaulted; a schoolteacher friend of Megan's who was slashed in the face by a gang of schoolkids and was now suffering from septicaemia after undergoing plastic surgery; a social worker thrashed by a child abuser; and an elderly man injured by a hit and run driver. There was a cot death, a teenage girl produced her baby in the ambulance, a Catholic woman slit her wrists after becoming pregnant by her brother-in-law and a small boy caught his penis in his trouser zip.

At a pinch the team were able to cope. But their lives were tough, as ever. Duffy was visited by the sister of her boyfriend Peter. The news was bad. Peter had died – though not from Aids. He had been involved in a road accident. Duffy tried to hide her grief until Charlie reprimanded her one day for sloppy work and the truth poured out. Cyril celebrated his success in exams by sporting new, blue rimmed specs and Kuba made earnest efforts to improve his English only to find himself made redundant in the cut-backs.

Megan had stopped wondering about giving up nursing even though continuing in Holby meant she must live on her own now that husband Ted worked in Cheltenham. In this series we watched her suffer from stress which made her physically ill – at one point she feared her cancer had returned. It also made her angry that as a relatively low-graded 'greenie' (green-uniformed SEN rather than the blue-uniformed SRN) she was ineligible for promotion to Sister, given the worst jobs and, to compound matters, she could not work in her homeland Ireland. 'Oh, yes, Megan Roach, Mother Superior, Mother soddin' earth!'

Mind you, after Megan poured out those bitter feelings to Ewart, her enduring strength was underlined. He left her to visit the observation ward he'd fought to stop being closed as an

Roy Kinnear, the much-loved actor who survived as a patient in Holby but died while making a film

economy. There he had a second heart attack and, despite the efforts of the team to revive him, died.

But by far the greatest tragedy to occur during this series was suffered by Roy Kinnear, the roly-poly comedy actor. While filming a movie in Spain in September, he fell from a horse and later died. His family demanded an investigation into the medical care he received there. At that time, he had already recorded scenes for *Casualty*'s episode seven, 'A Wing and a Prayer'. He played a fifty-year-old, Brian McCarthy, brought in with a suspected coronary, who luckily got the last available bed in Holby. It meant an eighty-year-old stroke victim had to lose out. Out of sympathy with Roy's widow and children the episode was postponed. It was finally shown in August 1989.

Series Four: New Symptoms, New Cures

After three years most viewers knew that the Holby A & E team did a hard, sometimes heart-breaking, job in a far from perfect National Health Service. What they hadn't learned to do was to play the *Casualty* game: spot the victim, guess the crisis. For this the show had to develop its potential to tease and thrill without losing its basic truthfulness.

It was a trick pulled off by a young Dubliner, Peter Norris, when he took over as producer in 1989. His arrival in Bristol had surprised no one as much as himself. Geraint Morris had been offered a chance to put his *Softly Softly* experience to work on the Thames police drama, *The Bill*, which was then moving from an hour-long show to a twice-weekly continuing series. It left Jonathan Powell with a problem. He cast around and found Peter Norris, who was completing an adaptation of the DH Lawrence classic *The Rainbow* as the production's assistant producer. *Casualty* couldn't have been more different and he had never produced a series before. But Jonathan needed to do no arm-twisting. 'I was on my way to Bristol like a shot,' Peter recalls.

There were no scripts and no cast at that stage. But Jonathan Powell had decided to experiment. *Casualty* would move to Fridays and to a later time, 9.30 p.m. after the so-called 'watershed'. 'The show was highly successful and I certainly wasn't going to change it out of all recognition,' says Peter Norris. 'I enjoyed the exotica of medicine very much but I guessed the audience could take things a bit tougher.'

For this he hired writers with bees in their bonnets about special issues. 'We allowed them freedom with the writing to tackle strong stories head on. The first three series had looked at the politics of the NHS. I cut back on that so that I'd have the chance to go in harder on individual

New girls Dr Lucy Perry (Tam Hoskyns) and nurse Alex Spencer (Belinda Davidson) have rough rides at first

social issues, terrorism, football hooliganism, charity fund-raising, racial violence, the lack of understanding for the mentally ill, and child prostitution and female circumcision which happens here, though few people know it.'

Peter also decided that Holby should not be Bristol under another name. It became a city anywhere in Britain and, accordingly, Duffy's West Country accent magically disappeared. Kuba was replaced by Jimmy Powell, who brought a Geordie voice to Holby and who was initially at least as carefree as his colleagues were careworn. He quickly became popular, especially with women viewers. Peter hired a casting director and, with script editor, Susan Gandar, devised new characters who included Dr Lucy Perry, the SHO, who was all books and brains but no practice and compassion; Alex Spencer, a middle-class student nurse; and Julie Stevens, a receptionist who liked to diagnose while she took down names and addresses.

Dr Andrew Bower (William Gaminara) came in as a registrar who was also dating Duffy. But, as in all good soap storylines, happiness cannot last (because it's boring). So when Duffy discovered

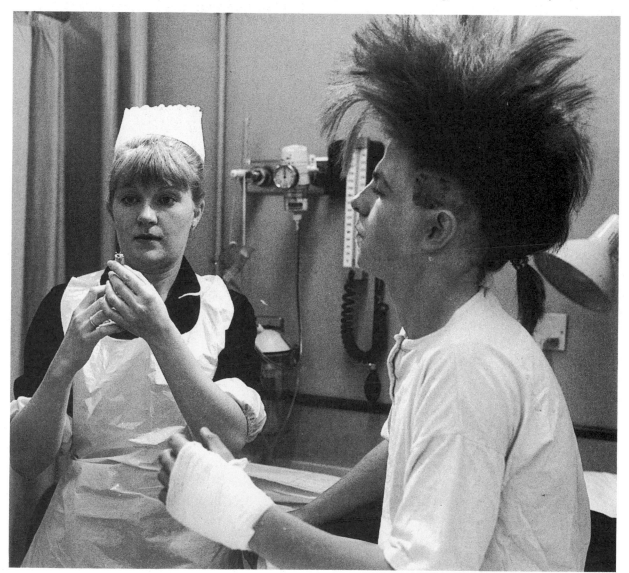

Sister Duffy (Catherine Shipton) prepares an injection of hair relaxant, or something

she was pregnant, she ended their relationship. Megan's problems continued. Ted had ended their 25-year-old marriage and she began taking tranquillisers until Charlie caught her red-handed at the drugs cupboard and talked her through things. She redeemed herself in everyone's eyes (with the possible exception of the Holby management) and became *Casualty*'s super-goodie when she spoke out to the press after staff shortages led to the death of a patient.

A spectacular road accident and a terrorist bomb exploding in a department store, series four's first and last episodes, are probably the most memorable. The first involved more vehicles than *Casualty* had ever used together before: two cars, two lorries, police cars, fire engines, ambulances and, rolling between them all, drums of hydrofluoric acid from one of the lorries. The story involved a teenage girl, stopped and questioned and then left by police as she stood

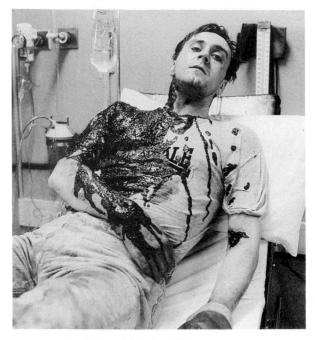

A builder (Joe McGann) falls into bitumen

Dr Julian Chapman (Nigel Le Vaillant) gave the team a hard time but found firm friends

hitch-hiking by the motorway. She was soon picked up by a pervert. When he lunged at her and lost control of his car, vehicles started careering and buckling. She went through the windscreen. The policeman who'd questioned her returned to the rescue but, overcome by fumes, fell and later died in agony from acid burns. Lucy and Cyril rushed to the scene and did what they could. It included lung surgery on the tarmac.

An irony was that some of the huge drums actually did cause a small accident. The crewman, whose job it was to push them into the mêlée, overdid it. A few drums hurtled towards the camera crew and everyone had to run for it. 'I heard the cameraman utter an oath and dart away only to return a second later to drag his equipment to safety,' Peter Norris recalls. 'A BBC Safety Officer was present and I was filling in forms for a year afterwards.'

The final episode turned out to be scheduled on the week of the remembrance service for the victims of the IRA bombing at Enniskillen. 'We were nervous but there were no protests. I think Geraint had won those battles. Political and public attitudes had caught up with *Casualty* by then. Looking back I was glad because making that episode had been a lark. Everyone was bloodspattered. Even the camera boom had a bandage on it. The place looked like the war scene from *Gone with the Wind*.'

The episodes in between weren't exactly tame, either. Perhaps the goriest sight was the monk who, it turned out, had been punishing himself by wearing a belt of nails. The humour darkened too in some stories. When a young man was brought in with head injuries Charlie advised him, 'Don't blow your nose or your brains will come out.'

The new night, later slot and strong stories didn't deter viewers. Far from it. Audiences grew to more than 13 million.

Series Five: Upping the dose

Casualty had never been about goodies versus baddies. Moral judgements have no place in an A & E ward. And if you wanted neat, wrapped-up endings, you watched another show. But in 1990 when Brenda Fricker went to Hollywood, came back with an Oscar for playing a woman who could have been Megan's poorer sister, the mother of crippled Christie Brown in *My Left Foot*, you couldn't help noticing that the Holby saints seemed to outnumber the Holby sinners. The regulars needed an anti-hero.

Happily, he had just arrived. Julian Chapman, Registrar, was arrogant, cold, the sort of doctor everyone knows and hates. Until he had to use his surgeon's skills and saved someone they love, that is.

With him in this new series, also produced by Peter Norris, was Beth Ramanee, an Indian

Dr Beth Ramanee (Mamta Kaash) became a favourite

Megan is sweet-talked by Tony Walker (Eamon Boland)

although born in Britain, caring and capable but as uncertain as any junior doctor might be. She and Julian were to fight and fight again. Each time she lost but viewers loved it.

There was a small new star too. Derek Thompson's son Charlie played Duffy's baby Peter. Coping with nursing shifts and her son proved exhausting for Duffy. Baby-minders let her down. Her mother (Doreen Mantle) grudgingly helped sometimes and Mr Right did not arrive. A candidate for that post seemed to turn up for Megan. But social worker Tony Walker turned out to be married and a rat. New staff nurse Martin Ashford was, by contrast, an angel.

And, as before, Peter Norris chose to go boldly, inviting viewers into hell holes – a football ground riot, a car race when drivers have been drinking, a careless grandfather who kills a child, a prisoner who has been raped, an unemployed man so jealous he kills – trusting that they would see them in the right moral light, as the horrific results of avoidable causes.

The series ended with an armed madman,

Holby not Hillsborough, but a riot on a football terrace is a tragedy wherever it happens

played by Kenneth Cranham, taking Megan hostage in crash and, finally, shooting Charlie who'd arrived dressed in Jimmy's porter's jumper to remove a corpse. It made a thrilling, end-of-series cliffhanger. Was it believable? 'A bit of non-reality never hurt anyone,' says Peter.

The episode which the producer remembers most clearly was Megan's other ordeal – when a woman attacked her with a knife. The crew were out on location on a housing estate. There was some pressure to get the scenes done as time had been lost when Brenda Fricker had been called to Hollywood to collect her award.

'The poor woman had just come back from Los Angeles, not having slept for about five days, having partied with every Irish American in California,' Peter jokes. 'The press had been on the phone non-stop and I knew photographers would turn up, wanting a picture of her. But

A deranged gunman (Kenneth Cranham) takes no orders from Charlie

she hadn't brought the actual Oscar on to the housing estate. So I sent my assistant to the nearest sports shop and she came back with this cheap, plastic trophy. If you look hard at the photos of Oscar-winner Brenda in her triumph – that's what she's holding up.'

Series Six: Holistic Treatment

They predicted that *Casualty* would collapse without Megan. It didn't. It grew up a bit more. Geraint Morris moved back into the driving seat. Invited by Peter Cregeen, then Head of BBC's Drama Series, to return to *Casualty* and to develop a big new project, Geraint inherited some of the story ideas created by Peter Norris (who went off to do something entirely different again — *The Darling Buds of May*). Perhaps the most important of these ideas was the character of student nurse Kelly Liddle.

'I knew that Brenda would leave,' says Peter. 'I honestly think she would have done so even if she hadn't had her success in *My Left Foot*. She'd done five hard years and wanted a break. The nurses were the lynchpins and so far almost all of them had been heroes. I thought we should see someone who fails.'

Kelly Liddle, played by Adie Allen (whom Peter Norris never met), was destined to fail so completely that she committed suicide.

But first the good news. Charlie survived the bullet wound in his chest. Little was said about it — just as little was said about Megan's absence — but devoted fans picked up a remark or two among the busy regulars. They knew both incidents had caused pain. Charlie was never again to be the cheeky chappie we first knew and yet again his love life was to be awkward and unsatisfactory. He seemed to find a soulmate in social worker Trish Baynes but things never worked out. Still, his heart and mind were unchanged. Duffy continued to survive motherhood, Staff Nurse Sandra (Maureen Beattie) arrived to the

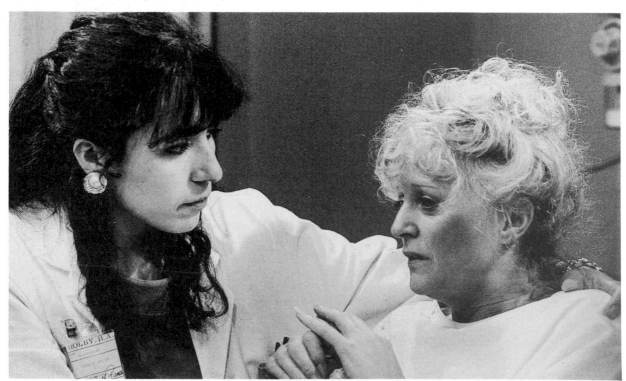

Dr Beth comforts a neurotic wife (Polly James)

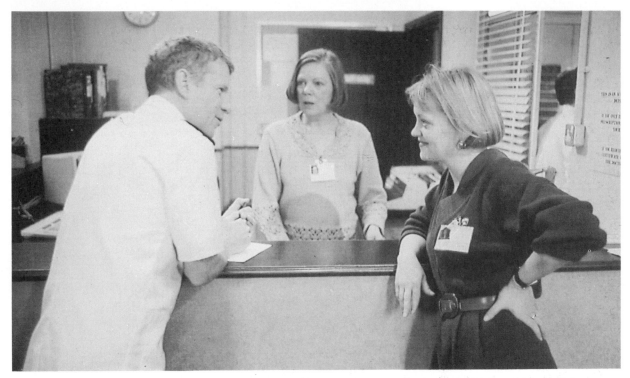

Even under the beady gaze of receptionist Norma (Anne Kristen) Charlie and Trish (Maria Friedman) become friends

delight of her growing legions of male fans. The character of nurse Ash (Patrick Robinson) was developed. He proved as sensitive as Sandra was sensible.

The doctors did not change in this series. Mamta Kaash had become so popular as Beth Ramanee that Geraint broke his rule of reflecting the A & E staff turnover. The scripts had her wanting to move on into general practice and Julian, who'd come to respect the junior he'd once criticized so easily, urging her to stay. It also had her following the wishes of one terminally ill man and not prolonging his life. The result was months of stress when a charge of negligence ensued. Julian also wanted to move – but up, not out. He used the old pals' act to assist him in winning promotion to the new post of Casualty Consultant. An important new-comer was Norma Sullivan, a seemingly snooty receptionist who'd rather you bled to death in front of her than failed to give your correct postcode for her paperwork. Anne Kristen had such an impact in the role that hospital receptionists everywhere wrote in protesting furiously.

For the third year running the show was screened at 9.30 p.m. on Fridays. Many squeamish viewers had long since learned to watch parts of *Casualty* with their eyes shut. But Geraint was still urged by his medical experts to be explicit about injury. 'They tell us that we must show the consequences of accidents, particularly those that can be avoided. We feel that showing that a thoughtless act on a cliff can mean something as permanent as amputation, or that mercy killings often have a tortured aftermath are justified. These things happen.'

Nurse Ashford (Patrick Robinson) and Dr Chapman are ready for the passengers when an airplane crashes

The thoughtlessness on a cliff formed the basis of the first episode. Nigel Le Vaillant, who played Julian, Catherine Shipton who is Duffy, and Caroline Webster, who plays paramedic Jane, agreed to do their own stunts in a massive rescue scene high above the Wye Valley. Nigel and Catherine were winched 200 feet from an RAF helicopter and Caroline, after just one day's training with the local rescue association, abseiled down 100 feet of rock face.

'The director asked me how my abseiling was,' she says, laughing. 'I thought it was a joke and said, "Marvellous". Then it dawned...' Nigel's reward was to saw off a young boy's

Paramedic Jane (Caroline Webster) abseils down a cliff to help an injured climber

injured foot. 'It was a piece of wood but it made me feel quite sick,' he admits. The episode not surprisingly drew more than 12 million viewers. By the last but one episode, 15.5 million viewers were hooked.

The final episode centred on an aircrash, a challenge for the designer Andrew Purcell. What no one spotted until they worked out on which Friday in December it was due to be screened was that it coincided with the third anniversary of that bizarre and dreadful crash at Lockerbie. To avoid offending the relatives of those who'd suffered it was pulled off and shown the following May.

Geraint and his team were disappointed. But not half as much as they were to be after the final episode of the next series.

Series Seven: Double Length, Extra Strength

By 1992 *Casualty* was almost too successful. The BBC not only wanted more of it, Jonathan Powell wanted much more of it, half-hour episodes twice a week, every week. 'It was a fantastic show by then,' he says. 'It cried out to be turned into a bi-weekly at eight o'clock like *The Bill*. It was too good an idea to miss. It would have boosted our audiences for the rest of those evenings and solved the problem of getting viewers back after *Coronation Street*. Everyone inside television thought that's what would happen. I'm pretty sure that's why ITV decided to run *The Bill* three times a week.

'So we started to plan for it. Geraint Morris was keen – all producers enjoy making changes and a successful bi-weekly is a terrific achieve-

The recession pushes one farmer tragically over the edge (Philip Whitchurch, Polly Hemingway and Max Danicic)

ment. The main actors were signed up too. Once we explained that things would not be done on the cheap, they were happy.' But John Birt, the BBC's Director General Designate, was not. 'He did not want two or more soaps in the schedules. So I had no alternative but to go with *Eldorado*, the Spanish soap, as a replacement for the *Wogan* show.'

Soon after *Eldorado* began in July 1992 it acquired the label 'the flop soap'. Its ratings were meagre and in March 1993 the decision was taken that it would end only one year after it began. By then Jonathan Powell had left the BBC to join Carlton Broadcasting. 'If *Casualty* had gone bi-weekly, I would have stayed [at the BBC],' he now says.

Geraint Morris was not opposed to turning *Casualty* into a twice-a-week, half-hour show. 'We did a feasibility study and it could have worked very well. But it would have been a very different *Casualty*. We'd have had to double up on everything. We've always been guided by our medical experts. The whole programme is worked around them. All our stories are based on fact. It takes time to get things right.'

The solution for the BBC was to make a much longer series, twenty-four episodes, which would effectively run for half the year. When those were repeated, as was planned, it would mean fans would be able to see their favourite medical team in action almost every week. And because it was so popular, the seventh series was to be shown on Saturdays again and at an earlier time, of around eight p.m.

Meanwhile *Casualty*'s advisors were warning the writers of the dangers of making their stories too cosy. When hospitals around Britain opted out and became Trusts there were problems. The senior staff were put under new pressure to hire and fire, juggle budgets and become managers as well as clinicians. There are even 'gagging

New Senior House Officer Rob Khalefa (Jason Riddington) buckles under the strain

clauses' written into contracts to stop them speaking out about worsening conditions. With millions of people suffering from the effects of the economic recession, there should be no soft soap in the BBC's most successful and respected drama series. The writers listened. As a result the new series won a record number of viewers, around 16 million, and the BBC's own research showed the 'audience appreciation' – a measurement of how much viewers enjoy the episodes they watch – was a record 82 per cent for almost every episode. But because it was hard-hitting, the series was also destined to get up people's noses and to catch a cold.

The subjects ranged from the gang rape of a rent boy, sexual abuse of children, surrogate pregnancy and organ donation to wife battering, a chilling nuclear power story, the grounding of a luxury yacht, a circus trapeze artist's spectacular fall and an horrific fall from an electricity

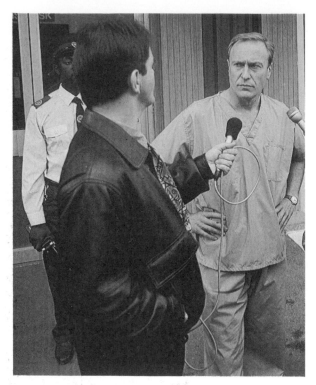

The Trust system doesn't suit consultant Julian Chapman. He protests to the press and quits

pylon. Finally, a story by Peter Bowker had rioting youths following the ambulances which came into their midst back to Holby and, crazily, setting the A & E department alight.

As usual the staff changed. A new public-school-educated SHO, Rob Khalefa (Jason Riddington) arrived and proved himself tactless, incompetent at times and willing to let a nurse carry the can when there were complaints. None of this mattered to the legions of teenage girls who swooned when he appeared, though. Chirpy, keen Maxine Price (Emma Bird) arrived as their new Health Care Assistant. Two new General Managers, one sympathetic, one not, arrived and the regular staff coped with the familiar problems of love and money. Ever-capable Nurse Ashford's work began to suffer when

he found it hard to meet his mortgage payments and his pretty girlfriend became pregnant and then opted for an abortion.

Nasty Norma's problem came to light: she was caring for a mother with Alzheimer's disease. Charlie buckled under the strain of the new Trust system. The business decisions made by the Holby management so outraged consultant Julian Chapman that he resigned. This was prompted partly by actor Nigel Le Vaillant's wish to leave the series to return to the theatre. He says, 'Chapman was never a rebel but he was amazed that decisions which ten years ago one wouldn't have thought possible started being made.' The final straw was his discovery that a piece of basic equipment for patients with broken spines could not be afforded but money was found to make the board room more lavish. Into the job came streetwise, sensible Dr Mike Barratt, played by Clive Mantle.

The series attracted a host of esteemed actors to take guest roles – even though they knew they'd look terrible: tear-stained at best, blood-spattered and bedraggled or dead at worst. It didn't deter Jan Harvey, Rula Lenska, Susan Penhaligon, Helen Lederer, Dora Bryan, Hywel Bennett, Amanda Redman, Jesse Birdsall and former *Coronation Street* star Shirin Taylor among many others. Maxine Audley also appeared shortly before her death – her last on-screen appearance.

The aah! quotient was supplied by the romance of stony-faced Julian Chapman and pale-eyed Nurse Sandra. And when Duffy's former boyfriend, Andrew Bower (William Gaminara), returned as the locum (filling in after Julian's abrupt departure) and warmly greeted a small boy only to be told he was Peter, his own son, a few million watching mums shared his delight.

On the second weekend in February 1993,

two-year-old Jamie Bulger was led away from his mother in a shopping mall in Liverpool by two older children. He was later found dead. Britain recoiled in horror and politicians and other self-appointed moral watchdogs asked how youngsters could be guilty of such senseless violence. An easy answer, which Prime Minister John Major and others quickly offered, was that young people are apt to copy the violent behaviour they watch on films and television.

There were protests about *Casualty's* 'Child's Play' episode, in which a young husband earns money as a rent boy. There were no scenes of rape, only of the young man's look of terror at a

It's been 'A Hard Day's Night' Julian and Sandra sing

Health Care Assistant Maxine Price (Emma Bird) is priceless with patients

gathering of older men. There were protests about 'Family Matters' which portrayed a family in which a father abuses his teenage son who in turn abuses his small sister. Under pressure, Alan Yentob, who succeeded Jonathan Powell, rescheduled the last episode, 'Boiling Point', to a later, 9.30 p.m. slot on 27 February. Before it began, an announcement was made: 'This episode features riot scenes of some power and impact.' It certainly did.

At a time when the press and TV news gave Jamie Bulger stories top billing and the nation seemed obsessed with the crimes of violent boys, the fictional young hooligans of Holby were thrown into the spotlight. There were a reported 700 protests from the 17.0 million

Charlie finally stops fighting his depression

viewers who watched 'Boiling Point'. Mrs Mary Whitehouse, the veteran TV 'clean-up' campaigner, mobilized publicity. Tory politicians shared their feelings of regret that scenes of youths rioting, fighting viciously, petrol-bombing and starting a fire at a hospital were shown at peak time. Under attack, on Channel 4's *Right to Reply*, controller, Alan Yentob, denied that the programme was promoting violence. 'However, I would say that on this occasion, *Casualty* and the *Casualty* team didn't get it right.'

Geraint Morris was understandably disappointed at the outcries. 'It seemed clear to me that the episode was dealing with the tragic consequences of violent acts. The moral was plain. As usual, those who wish to bash the BBC are very well-organized. I think the viewing figures and audience appreciation figures vindicate us entirely. Even then, I am surprised that anyone believes these things do not happen for real.'

His views are echoed by the Leeds-based writer of 'Boiling Point', Peter Bowker, a man who had taught young adults with learning difficulties for many years before taking up scriptwriting. He based the episode's events on personal experience. Months before, a group of teenage boys had kicked down his own front door one evening while he was at home. They announced themselves as 'the Mafia' before grabbing valuables. They had already broken into several other houses on the estate. He called the police who said they didn't send officers into those situations because resources were limited. Shortly after this incident his girlfriend was pelted with stones by a gang of boys in the street. She grabbed one by his hand. At this point the boy's mother appeared and beat her up.

'The violence was having a completely corrupting effect on me,' he confesses. 'I was keeping a tyre iron by my front door. The kids had become hooked on the power of their violence. They weren't really interested in stealing. As a result there was talk locally of our forming a protection group. That's how vigilante organisations are formed. People feel so vulnerable. I did.'

He began to research and found several documented cases where youths had followed ambulances back to hospitals and set fire to rubbish bags with serious consequences. They regarded the ambulance staff as intruders, informers. Peter Salt added his experiences of the mindless violence of those who follow casualties into hospital. 'In these instances there's no such thing as the last word,' adds Peter Bowker. 'I hoped "Boiling Point" would be seen as a deeply moral piece. I know from experience that kids relate to characters like Duffy and Ash. That's why I had the son of a knifed man talking to Ash. I wrote the attacks in a purely negative way. To me

As Holby is set alight, the *Casualty* team battle on

Casualty is at the moral centre of BBC drama. To attack it is beyond my moral universe. I think it has been deliberately misread.'

As a result the planned repeat of the series was postponed. Only selected episodes were reshown in the spring of 1993, to the dismay of the cast who felt badly let-down. Among the viewers who were more distressed by this than by the allegedly strong scenes in 'Boiling Point' were youths and young adults with learning and behavioural problems who lived in a residential care centre in Yorkshire. Mrs Rosemary Cusick, who runs the centre, contacted BBC1's *Points of View* to report that the people there had indeed been horrified by the events in 'Boiling Point'. They had realized for the first time that starting a rumpus, as a lark, could escalate into riots, destruction and deaths. The work of heroes such as Charlie and Duffy could be wrecked. After viewing that final episode of the most popular-ever series of *Casualty* her residents had discussed these matters. Mrs Cusick felt they had learned from it. They were surely not alone.

In May, a complaint to the Broadcasting Standards Council from 55 viewers about the unacceptable level of violence in 'Boiling Point' was upheld. It provoked several debates in the media about screen violence. In July, *Radio Times* published a selection of readers' letters. One, from Mrs McKeown of Eastbourne, Sussex, included this thought:

'Of course, gratuitous violence on TV is alarming but the episode of *Casualty* that was singled out actually made clear how mindless behaviour can escalate into tragedy.

'At least one young offenders' group that I know of was shown it and was appalled to see what can happen. Thus it was a learning experience and did only good.'

Is this the end of Holby?

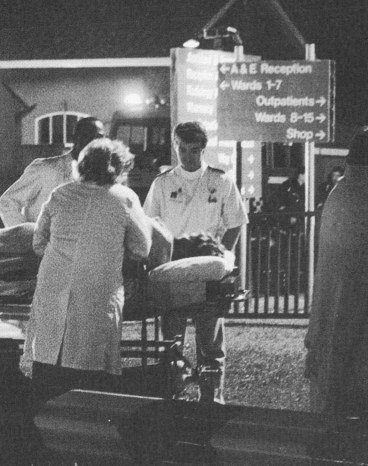

WHO'S WHO IN HOLBY

Casualty characters have always been quirky, different. The staff aren't models of patience and the patients aren't models of anything except perhaps human weakness. You'll find sketches of the regular nurses, the important doctors and other favourite staff here with the gen about the actors who play them.

Nurses

CHARLIE FAIRHEAD

Once upon a time, Charlie Fairhead used to be a nice young curly-haired bloke who liked girls, snooker, a smoke, wearing a sheepskin flying jacket and driving his battered car. He kept in touch with his mum, who had arthritis and thought the world of him. As for work, well, oddly enough, he got satisfaction and a few laughs from being a nurse – Charge Nurse actually, equal to a Sister, a boss to the others except in medical judgements where the doctors, often women doctors, wore the trousers. And if you thought that was cissy, that was your problem. Charlie had a great sense of humour and a terrible temper. He'd stand with his hands in his pockets and, when people asked the impossible, rub the back of his head, look into the middle distance and wince.

Eight years on and he's still doing it. He's a little thinner, greyer and more serious, weighed down with the responsibility of running a large department, handling a huge budget, and helping patients who are as foolish and unlucky as ever they were. These days Charlie's a Clinical Nursing Manager. It's more money but he's too tired to spend it.

When consultant Ewart Plimmer died Charlie took on the job of fighting for the department's existence and he has battled with administrators over staff, beds and equipment ever since. He's fair, unselfish. It's no wonder his nurses don't moan about him. They only moan with him. With the doctors he's straightforward, adaptable, bright – so long as they don't ask him to approve of transplants. When a young man's organs became available, Charlie accused Beth and Julian of body-snatching.

The part of the job he hates most is being a bouncer when drunks and troublemakers cause a rumpus. But he can be brave, as he showed when he tried to rescue Megan, who was being held at gunpoint by a madman. It earned him a bullet in the chest. He didn't brag when he returned for series six. He was a bit unsteady on his feet, that's all. And you just knew he'd been a rotten patient.

Other people's most private problems he can cope with. His own baffle him. Even choosing a car. Remember the clapped out Beetle, the rusting heap of a jeep? Charlie planned to buy a smart, reliable motor when he won some money on the Premium Bonds. Being Charlie, he spent it on a private hip operation for his mum instead.

With women friends, he never gets it right. Dr Baz loved him and left him, after aborting his baby. Nurse Karen O'Malley sensed he wasn't serious and gave up. Administrator Valerie Sinclair liked him but they were fighting on opposite sides at work. Social worker Trish liked him a lot but discovered he had feet of clay.

Over the years we've watched Charlie (he has appeared in all but two episodes) and wondered

if perhaps he hankered after Duffy. Was there something more than the bond of mutual respect and friendship between them? They've seen each other through their worst moments. She helped him when his drinking became a problem in series five, and tried to steer him to a therapist when depression numbed him in series seven. They've confided in each other. Twice he has persuaded her not to quit. In 'Silent Night' they kissed under the mistletoe in the car park and … and … ? Nothing. She married another. If there is a perfect partner out there for Charlie, she'd better not be in a hurry. Charlie Fairhead's so open-minded that knowing his own mind is very hard work.

Derek Thompson

It's a bit weird talking to Derek Thompson. He looks you straight in the eye, doesn't rub the back of his head and draws fanciful pictures with words, captioning them with wry irreverent jokes. Charlie Fairhead, the man he has developed to become Britain's most dedicated, professional male nurse, hasn't time for such luxuries. Also he's shy, hence the awkward glances.

'Charlie's a good character to underplay,' Derek says. 'I try to make him someone who doesn't think he's being watched. That's why he is a hero.'

It took Derek a while to get to understand his hero. Then ten minutes into the first studio session, back in 1986, there was, he says, a 'lightbulb moment' as he watched Peter Salt, the Bristol Royal

Infirmary Clinical Nursing Manager on whom Charlie is based.

'I saw Peter walking through this highly charged studio, a situation that was quite new to him, and he was doing what he does as a nurse, being calm and rational when everyone else was being emotional. It suddenly struck me that for him the ear is as important as the eye, he was absorbing all the information. The calm exterior is his way of making it plain that he's not about to pass judgement on any of the personal, intimate details of other people's lives he trips over.'

Since then Peter and Derek have become firm friends. 'He's a plain man, not the least bit secretive or devious. But I don't impersonate him. I take the nuts and bolts of nursing from him. Charlie's personal affairs are inventions.'

Belfast-born Derek's career started when his engineer father, a keen semi-pro singer who had toured the variety theatres, encouraged the boy and his twin sister Elaine to practise a song and dance act. At the age of eleven they appeared on stage and made their first record, *One Little Robin in a Cherry Tree*. At twelve they did a spot on the *Billy Cotton Band Show* for television. He was acting at the same time too, he reckons. 'When I made a mistake in the harmony, I would look at Elaine in a way that made everyone think it was her fault!' he laughs.

The family moved to London and the twins attended stage school as well as continuing their now successful act. But after Elaine teamed up with a bandleader,

Derek decided to strike out on his own, joined a repertory company and began a distinguished career which includes major stage roles, work at the National Theatre, parts in such films as *Yanks*, *The Long Good Friday* and *Breaking Glass* as well as TV roles such as Detective Sergeant Jimmy Fenton in *The Gentle Touch*. The authentic Northern Irish accent that Derek has used for many roles is much admired by other actors,

For a while Derek seemed to play only sinister young thugs and cornered the market in playing IRA soldiers. No politician protested.

including Marlon Brando who asked him to make a tape of it so he could try to copy it in a film.

For a while Derek seemed to play only sinister young thugs and cornered the market in playing IRA soldiers. 'No politician protested. Ironically I never had a bad reaction from anyone who watched. Even when I kidnapped a woman in *The Price* and ended up chopping off one of her fingers, there wasn't a stir. Yet after a few episodes of playing a caring charge nurse in *Casualty*, questions were being asked in the Houses of Parliament and we were being accused of making left-wing

propaganda! Absurd!

'I still get a fair amount of Charlie-bashing from ex-professionals of the old school. They see him as a slovenly character, hands in pockets and all that, who tends to be on first-name terms with junior staff. But I also get a lot of letters from student nurses thanking me for taking the sting out of A & E.'

Now in his forties, Derek lives with actress Dee Sadler, whom he met when she played a pot-holer in need of some Holby TLC in 'Lifelines'. (She also appeared in the episode 'All's Fair'.) 'I dragged Dee out of a horrible cave in the Cheddar Gorge and bought her lunch – what more could she want?' Derek jokes. Dee settled with him in Bristol and he hasn't been down any more potholes – his hobbies are carpentry, walking, boating and playing musical instruments. Their baby, named Charlie, was born in 1989 and played Duffy's son Peter in the early years. 'He loves the notion that I'm a Charlie too and I'm in *Casualty*, which he has seen bits of. He likes to tease me.'

As a former Equity union representative Derek sympathised when Charlie wore a NUPE shop steward hat. He adds that he's delighted to be linked with a drama that 'points up some unpalatable truths' about the health service. As someone who almost died of pneumonia as a child and has suffered occasionally serious asthma attacks since, he is a passionate supporter of a well-funded NHS.

'On one occasion with the asthma I was crawling around the

flat for a couple of days, not making a lot of sense because of the lack of oxygen reaching my brain. When I was finally taken into the Bristol Royal Infirmary, it was doubly reassuring to hear the language that I understood and to see them all working the way we do on *Casualty*.'

Being involved for eight years now with other people's pain – albeit pretend pain – is sometimes wearing, he admits. 'As an actor you have no control and the anxiety and distress do get to me. But Charlie's personal problems come off with the white coat at the end of the day's filming. That's why Charlie's depression last year was fun. I didn't like looking a mess. But I enjoyed the breakdown. I imagined a piece of plutonium in the back of my head.'

Derek smiles at the memory of Charlie's long list of failed romances and is eagerly awaiting reaction to the character's painful dilemma in the 1993 series. 'I felt sure the relationship with Trish Baynes was going to develop into marriage and babies and so did Maria Friedman who played her. I was looking forward to it. But I think the writers wanted to make a point about the loneliness or perhaps the lone-ness of the man.'

Would he ever quit? 'Sure, if I got fed up. But I never do. I have a ball on *Casualty*.'

LISA DUFFIN
Newly qualified State Registered Nurse Lisa 'Duffy' Duffin fancied the job on Holby's permanent night shift when it came up, back in 1986. She knew there'd be a

strong team spirit (stronger than on other wards where the staff worked a shift rota) and she thought it would be exciting. Probably her horoscope helped her decide to say 'yes'.

In those days local girl Duffy didn't take her work that seriously. Not as seriously as, say, losing a few pounds so she could fit into a new outfit, passing her driving test or sharing a laugh with her pal Susie, the receptionist, about the ward's not-so-secret lovers Ponting and Mute and Charlie and Baz. She found there were issues to fight for, though, when a cinema started showing 'naughty nurse' porno films, Duffy staged a demonstration and scored a success.

At that time Duffy lived alone in a damp flat with her two cats but was always cheerful. Until the night she was raped in a dark back street on her way to work, that is. She didn't go to the police but later wished she had. Susie, Megan and Ewart helped her through it. She tries to follow suit by supporting patients who've suffered in the same way.

Promoted to Staff Nurse, Duffy also became knowledgeable and thoughtful with patients who were HIV positive, again because she'd been there. Her first proper boyfriend Peter Tranter (played by Eric Deacon), a salesman, was set to whisk her to America before he found out he had the Aids virus. She took a test too. It was negative but the affair was over. Peter became a recluse and later she learned he'd died. Dashing Dr Andrew Bower took her mind off it all. Then Duffy found she was

pregnant. She also found out how much her job – she'd just been promoted to Sister – meant to her. Could she work with a baby? She decided she'd try but that she didn't want Andrew. She had second, third and fourth thoughts on that. When baby Peter was born, the joys of motherhood were often dimmed by the struggle to do it all, especially when babyminders let her down and the baby had to come to work too. Her somewhat self-centred mother (played by Doreen Mantle) was no help at first. She disapproved, thought Duffy should give up her job. Then she rallied round. In 1991, new boyfriend Paul Slater (played by William Armstrong), who had his own electrical business, persuaded her to move in with him. He was fine with baby Peter but no friend of Holby Hospital – he wanted Duffy to leave. In the event she left him.

By now, the once daffy Duffy had days as huffy, stuffy Duffy. She picked fault with Student Nurse Alex, clashed with porter Jimmy Powell, was a tartar with Student Nurse Kelly and a tough boss to Health Care Assistant Max. Dr Rob Khalefa was on the receiving end of her icy looks too. We understood the pressures. And when her health became the worry in 1992, we forgave Duffy everything. She was called back after a routine smear test – was it cervical cancer? Should she jump a long queue for the next test to find out? She thought not, but her pal Sandra Nicholl told Julian Chapman. He had no qualms about pulling strings and the

news, when it came, was good.

Then came another shock. When he left Holby, Julian's temporary replacement was Andrew Bower. Nervously, Duffy agreed to let him see Peter. He was captivated. He didn't get the permanent job but he'd found Duffy again. Sandra said 'go for it'. They planned a quiet wedding. On the night before, Duffy didn't

Then Duffy found she was pregnant. She also found out how much her job meant to her.

get an early night and sweet dreams, though. Rioting youths burned the department to the ground. Duffy, soot-smeared and weeping, seemed to lose heart for the very first time.

Catherine Shipton
Struggling young actress Catherine Shipton had to hobble to her audition for the role of Duffy on 11 January 1986. Her agent had put her up for the part of Susie, the receptionist. But Catherine fancied the nurse role, partly because so many people had told her she looked like a nurse, and partly because she liked the fact that Duffy was obsessed with losing weight and with astrology. Just as she herself was. But she wasn't hopeful. She thought her

bandaged sprained ankle would put the kybosh on her chances.

In fact, it clinched it. 'The day before I'd been teaching aerobics – one of the ways I kept the wolf from the door – I'd fallen and had to go to casualty to be strapped up,' she says. 'I was trying to hide that leg at the interview but Geraint Morris and the writers there were fascinated. "Let's see how they did it. What was the nurse like?" they asked me. I told them she was bad-tempered, stressed and had told me it was my own silly fault. They were intrigued.' Catherine was hired.

Catherine, born in Lewisham, South London, in 1957, was more than pleased. She was saved. She had been on the point of throwing up acting and returning to university after a rotten year. For the first time since leaving drama school five years earlier, she'd regretted taking the advice of a tutor who, having watched her in a students' Shakespeare effort, urged her to switch from her languages degree course. Worst of all, her father had died suddenly that year after a heart attack. 'I'd talked to him on the telephone at ten and he was dead by midnight,' she recalls. 'I'd forced my mother to tell me exactly what had happened, what had been tried on dad at the hospital.' In 1992 Duffy had to try to resuscitate an elderly couple in a *Casualty* episode. 'What I had to do as an actress was so similar, it all came back to me and I couldn't do it.'

Playing Duffy has changed Catherine's fortunes and made her pretty, if not perfect, face one of

the country's favourites. One of the things her fans (though not cameramen) most like, it seems, is her sticky-out right ear which her mum, she says, used to try to pin back with Sellotape.

Catherine's satisfaction developed with the character. At the start Duffy was 'a kidney bowl carrier, a blue flash', little more. But at the end of the first series, after the sexual attack, there was a turning point. The cheeky girl started to have an emotional life. Later, when she had the baby and became a Sister, there was another gear change. 'I think lots of women who juggle a job and bringing up a child identified with her. And I had the chance to show that nurses are professionals, not dogsbodies or angels or girls desperate to find a doctor to marry

And I had the chance to show that nurses are professionals not dogsbodies or angels.

them. I've been in every episode and I've loved every minute.'

Catherine has changed, too. The much admired, long, reddish-blonde hair is the same. But there's less of the actress. In 1992 she lost around a stone and a half when she stopped slavishly following diets. She feels she has been educated by the scripts and the letters from

viewers. After Duffy's sexual assault, girls and women poured their hearts out in letters to her, some having suffered silently for years until then. There have been the letters from sick people which made her weep, like one from a fourteen-year-old who'd just been told she had multiple sclerosis. The more she saw how real medical staff work (like most of the cast, Catherine has been a fly on the BRI wall from time to time), the harder she found it was to act.

'You want to do the job right, to go for the truth. I always do my own suturing, for instance. It makes me feel like a nurse. But sometimes the script really gets to us. New actors who come in often can't believe how low they feel after a few weeks. I think it's the verbal and physical abuse they have to take. It doesn't help that we know we can go home at the end of the day, forget about it and we'll be paid much, much more than if we were doing it for real.'

Now, after eight years, Catherine has decided to hang up her bedpan. 'In 1991 I went on holiday to the Maldives and as I relaxed the idea came through that after the next year I should be going. So I'll be leaving during this new series. Duffy won't meet a grisly end or anything like that, so she could always come back. But I want to try to practise my craft out of a blue frock.'

Catherine hopes to work on stage, try some comedy and film a four-part television drama that has been written for her, the story of a woman leading a humdrum life. Holby will never be quite the same.

MARTIN ASHFORD

Senior Staff Nurse Martin 'Ash' Ashford was a bit impatient sometimes. But he had principles, dreams. No one was keener. He did every task by the book and he did them well. He still does. He deserved his promotion in 1992 and would have deserved another to Clinical Nurse Specialist if Ken Hodges hadn't also applied for the job and got it because he had that little bit more experience. Ash is niggled about it. He can't help it. He thought Charlie was a friend as well as a boss.

All in all, life hasn't been kind lately. The mortgage on his small studio flat leaves little cash for fun. His student girlfriend Nikki (Imogen Boorman) and he have split. After she had an abortion in 1992, the relationship died. He

still worries about his headstrong sister who bickers with their mother. He's still the union rep, but what power do unions have now? Not much. He's also diabetic, which can bring other strains. Even when Ash spends his hard-earned money on a night at a club, as he does in the new series, he has to help people and ends up back at Holby.

Patrick Robinson

When he was fifteen, Patrick Robinson's future was a toss-up. Heads he went to Southampton Football Club for a trial. Tails he stayed at school that day for a drama class. He said 'no' to football and now watches pals who played with him in the school team, and his cousin Ian Wright, on *Match of the Day*. He hasn't regretted his

choice. The charming six-foot-tall Londoner, the fifth of the seven children of a Jamaican bus-driver who brought up his family single-handed after their mother left, still plays football with pros and ex-pros for charity. He's also a serious roller skater and organizes street hockey on skates for London youngsters. His team, the Ashmead Cruisers, are almost unbeatable.

Patrick went to drama school after working in the offices of impresario Robert Stigwood. When he left he was snapped up by the Royal Shakespeare Company who made him Britain's first black Romeo. He played other classic roles there and toured Africa with a theatre company in 1990. 'Returning to chilly Britain just before Christmas, I was fed up. I thought I was about to learn the truth about actors "resting",' he says. Then the call came from *Casualty*, his first television role. 'Until Steven Spielberg calls for me I'm delighted to go on playing Ash,' he says.

Unlike his capable character, Patrick hates hospitals and refuses to be ill in case he needs to go near one. When his social worker partner Janis gave birth to their baby Charlotte two years ago, he braved it, though. 'It was different. Janis was the focus. Anyway I knew I had to get used to it. I'd like heaps of kids.'

ADELE BECKFORD

Like Sandra Nicholl, whom she replaces in series eight, Staff Nurse Adele Beckford is cheerful and efficient. She's returning to full-time work after raising her children. She's married to a cabinet-maker, her sons Tony and Curtis are at college and she's a busy bee in her local community, a familiar face at the church. Adele can size up the patients quickly and takes no nonsense from them. She also sees the funny side of events. That's why Charlie and Duffy, who know her from her part-time work on other wards, are pleased to have her back.

Doña Croll

Doña Croll knew she would enjoy joining the *Casualty* team before she began rehearsals early in 1993. A few years ago she appeared as a social worker who cut her wrist and came to Holby. 'So I knew what I was letting myself in for,' says the Birmingham actress viewers know from the comedy *Us Girls* and from last year's award-winning Screen Two film *Halleluyah Anyhow.*

This is Doña's first long-term role. She took it after discovering that, with many filming days during weekends, she could still spend part of her week in London with her young daughter Charlie. On occasion Charlie has accompanied her to Bristol and even got in on the act, playing a patient in the waiting room.

Doña originally planned to be a linguist but acting was an option from the time she played Bottom in her school's production of *A Midsummer Night's Dream.* After drama school she went to the Bush Theatre, was the first black Cleopatra at the Liverpool Everyman and took a lead role in *Serious Money* in the West End. And Adele has played a nurse before – in *EastEnders* she treated alcoholic Angie's kidney failure and had stern words with Dirty Den.

HELEN CHATSWORTH

Student Nurse Helen Chatsworth has studied for eighteen months on the Project 2000 nurse training scheme before she arrives at Holby in series eight. She's good at quoting from the text books and wants to analyse the patients but is hopeless with real emergencies. When she sees a girl of her own age with a badly gashed leg, she freezes and has to be led away. She drives placid Staff Nurse Adele mad with endless questions. She has ideas and suggestions, some good, some cheeky. But she has no tact. She almost asks to be tipped into the sluice. Helen is bright and basically well-meaning. But ahead of her is a year's worth of

struggles, mistakes and bouncing back.

Samantha Edmonds

It makes a change for pretty freckle-faced blonde Samantha Edmonds to appear on television looking clean. As art student Jo in *Teenage Health Freak* she used to rub her hands in pot plant soil and streak her face with paint before the cameras rolled. Now in her white tunic and trousers, she reckons she's almost unrecognisable. Londoner Sam,

who's dyslexic, went to drama classes as an escape from other book-based classes at school and grew to like acting. She moved on to drama school and won a role in *To Kill A Mockingbird* at the Mermaid in her last months there. Soon afterwards it seemed as though

Hollywood was knocking at the door when Sam was cast to play Richard Chamberlain's daughter in a mini-series. Sadly the star pulled out and Martin Sheen took over, giving Sam's role to his own daughter. There was a consolation, however. Sam was then free to play Harry Enfield's girlfriend and wife in *Gone to the Dogs* on ITV.

KENNETH HODGES

While Ken Hodges was studying to become a doctor, he decided to travel around Australia for a few years. He returned, took up nursing and qualified in 1986. Now home in Holby, he inadvertently upsets Ash when he joins the A & E team as the Clinical Nurse Specialist in series eight – Ash wanted the job himself. Ken also makes Charlie feel ill at ease for a while. Duffy soon realises that Ken is gay. He's not limp-wristed but the new porter Frankie Drummer makes him the butt of crude jokes. Will these wear him down? Or will administrator Mark Calder, who believes a CNS is a luxury the department should do without, blunt his enthusiasm?

Christopher Guard

So many good roles came his way that Christopher Guard kept postponing taking up his place to read English at Oxford. A child actor who, among other things, played the young David Copperfield in the BBC serial at the age of twelve, he had the pick of stage and television roles when he was young. After a spell as a lead in *A Little Night Music*, Chris joined

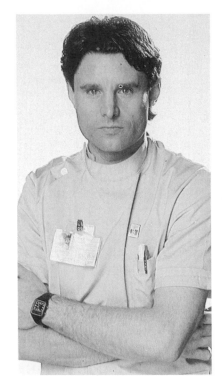

the National Theatre when he was twenty and said goodbye to his formal education.

He appeared in television series including *A Woman of Substance*, *My Cousin Rachel* and *Return to Treasure Island* and has also worked as a musician. Until recently his partner was actress Lesley Dunlop. Christopher now shares the job of bringing up their daughters Daisy and Rosie. 'I thought hard before I accepted the role of Ken,' says Chris. 'He's someone whose life is quite outside my experience but we're not making any great statement by including a man who happens to be gay. I've played a doctor in *The True Story of Dr Frankenstein* and medical techniques fascinate me. I like the fact that *Casualty* gets those things right.'

SANDRA NICHOLL

Even at Holby, women need to adjust their stocking tops from time to time. But when Sandra Nicholl hastily pulled up her staff nurse's uniform to do this once when she thought no one was looking, large numbers of male viewers went into shock. Had her admirer Julian Chapman been around, he might have added to their number. She has such fine legs, you see. Scottish Sandra was, however, no flibbertigibbet. She liked men but she was no tease.

Married to David who worked on oil rigs, Sandra had returned to nursing work in 1991 when her daughter Laura reached school age. She needed the work as much for the company as for the money. The Holby team knew her of old, knew she was efficient, brisk and could be tough. Sadly, she wasn't tough enough when the wet-behind-the-ears houseman Rob Khalefa urged her to set up a patient's drip. Then he left her to face a complaints inquiry on her own when the man suffered side effects. A less mature woman might have let it rankle but Sandra's sense of humour carried her through. Anyway, by then she was busy – turning Julian Chapman into a human being. When he quit the hospital and wanted her to live with him, she seemed to wake up from a pleasant dream to a difficult reality. Sandra decided to confess to her husband, try to stay with him and build a home for her daughter. After twenty-nine episodes, we'll miss her.

Maureen Beattie

When the writers closed the bedroom door on the morning of passion at her screen lover Julian's flat, Maureen Beattie was grateful. 'I think we'd seen enough pink things wobbling about in *Casualty* without that!' she jokes. She loved the screen affair and, when Nigel Le Vaillant left the cast, Maureen made him an intricately iced cake. In it the figure of Julian in his surgeon's greens could be seen sitting in a large oyster eating the shellfish and drinking the champagne that are Nigel's favourites.

Maureen, of the pale blue eyes and interesting stockings, is the daughter of Glasgow comic Johnny Beattie and sister of *Naked Video* star Louise. On leaving school she took a job as a lab technician in a veterinary college before attending the Scottish RADA, where she won the Gold Medal. Stage work followed and she has appeared in several television dramas including *Taggart*, *The Bill*, *Boon* and *My Dead*

Dad, in which she played a transsexual barmaid. Since leaving *Casualty* last year Maureen has returned to the stage and is completing a romantic novel.

She enjoyed Sandra's switch from a body who said little more than 'atrophine, doctor' to warm-blooded woman. The hardest thing was filming Sandra and Julian's duet at the karaoke night without laughing. 'The director made us sing the whole number,' she recalls. 'And our first kiss was agony. We did it at about seven thirty one morning and I felt I looked like the wreck of the Hesperus.'

She laughs at her 'sexy' nurse image. 'I had several letters, including marriage proposals, but I said "no".' Far more embarrassing was her one sortie in a borrowed nurse's uniform after a request to help raise funds at a charity event for National Transplant Week. The Lord Provost of Glasgow, among others, assumed she'd understand the technicalities of transplants, not recognizing her from *Casualty*.

'He asked me a series of questions I couldn't answer. I can just imagine him thinking what a waste of money it is to train nurses who end up not knowing the simplest thing!'

MEGAN ROACH

The Mother Earth of *Casualty* for its first five years, Megan Roach ruefully observed that she was just 'part of the furniture'. If so, she was the human part.

Frumpy, overweight, Irish and in her late forties, she was a favourite with everyone who

watched. The most experienced member of the nursing staff yet the least technically qualified, it irked Megan that as a lowly 'greenie', a State Enrolled Nurse, she could not be promoted. She was the one who did the dirty work – cleaned up the puddles and broke the saddest news to relatives.

Megan was, more than anyone else, a workhorse. She cooked and cleaned for her taxi-driver husband Ted (Nigel Anthony), her three grown-up sons Dave, Bernard and Tom, and her dog Oliver. Then at night she came to work. Ewart Plimmer and Charlie often relied on her to cajole ward sisters into finding empty beds where none had been found before. She could plead as well as she could sympathize, which she did with almost all of her patients. Doctors, like brusque young David Rowe, were another matter. They could put her down and she would bite her lip.

In the first series Megan was a patient as well as a nurse, undergoing a hysterectomy as treatment for cancer. Kuba came to visit her and twittered on about his own problems. Duffy called and told her she'd been sexually attacked. It was the trigger for Megan, with enough on her plate already, to let go and cry. It was also the start of a close friendship between the two women. Only once, in series four, when Duffy snapped that Megan couldn't let go of patients, was there ever a rift between them.

By 1988 Megan was cracking up. She knew her long marriage

was on the rocks. Ted was in Cheltenham, trying to find work. Increasingly dependent on tranquillisers stolen from work, she was lonely and isolated in her council flat. When she argued with a sixteen-year-old who was annoying her and stormed out of the cubicle, the department was aghast. Ewart played the stern father. The pill-taking stopped and the sense of humour returned.

On the day Julian Chapman arrived in 1990, Megan was late for work. She'd been to Ted's funeral. But social worker Tony Walker lifted her spirits and they soon fell in love. Was he too superficial, too young, too married? He seemed all three. He took a job in Manchester and asked Megan to join him. In her final episode, she was held hostage by a madman and saw Charlie get shot. Perhaps she decided Manchester had to be a better bet. Either way, Holby survived her leaving. Nurses do leave, after all. Wherever Megan is, she's sure to be busy humouring and helping people. Lucky people.

Brenda Fricker
Before there was Megan there was Brenda Fricker. Director Paul Unwin, one of the show's creators, had worked with the Dublin-born actress at the Bristol Old Vic when she played the lead in *Typhoid Mary*. 'She was tremendous. I talked to Geraint Morris about her and then to her. We knew the show had to have compassion. We made Megan, the person everyone could talk to, fit Brenda,' he says.

In reality, the two women are poles apart. 'Megan was the mother we all want, full of love and understanding. I'm none of that. I'm not a mother and never will be and I wasn't a very good wife,' says Brenda. 'I'm not even a good nurse to my father now he's old and frail. I'm much more rebellious than Megan. I couldn't do her job, ever. Just go down to the hospital and watch what they do for an eighth of the salary I earned pretending to be a nurse. It makes you blush. You break your heart with people being kicked in the teeth by life. I couldn't handle it. I'd be reduced to tears.'

Brenda Fricker is the daughter of a journalist. At nineteen she was assistant to the art editor of The Irish Times, hoping to become a reporter. Acting happened by chance. A call from a radio producer, who'd picked her at school for a child's part, brought the offer of a role in a Coronation Street-type series – Tolka Row, for Eire TV. Her newspaper boss said 'try it for six months' and she did.

Brenda became the Emerald Isle's best-loved character actress. Before Casualty she worked in the theatre and took the lead in the award-winning television film Ballroom of Romance. Between Casualty series, she made films such as The Field, UTZ, To Have and to Hold and My Left Foot (opposite Daniel Day Lewis), for which she won an Oscar for Best Supporting Actress. Since leaving Casualty in 1991, Brenda has appeared in Home Alone 2, made the Australian television series Brides of Christ, ITV's Seekers and two comedy films, So I Married

an Axe Murderer and Deadly Advice.

She may not have chosen to work in hospitals but Brenda has experienced plenty of them as a patient. At fourteen she was so badly injured in a car crash that she was laid up for two years. Soon after her discharge she contracted TB and spent two years in a sanatorium. She had several miscarriages during her marriage to director Barry Davies. And during the series in which Megan was attacked by a nutcase Brenda was twice attacked in the street. In

Megan was the mother we all want.

the second scramble youths cut her head so badly with a penknife she needed to have her head shaved. Strangely, no viewer spotted that her usual fair curls had been replaced by a wig.

Like Megan, Brenda has suffered from depression. 'I've spent months in psychiatric hospitals and I've talked to psychiatrists. But eventually you have to find your own strengths. My depression comes on like a cold for no apparent reason. It lasts for days and the only way I can handle it is to go underground, not answer the phone or the door.'

Although she admits that Casualty made her a visible star she believes she would have quit anyway, Oscar or no Oscar. 'Megan didn't develop in the way she was meant

to. She started off with a wonderful sense of humour. But she lost it and all she ever seemed to do was push a trolley round and offer tea and sympathy.'

Brenda now lives alone in Bristol with her dogs and enjoys drinking Guinness, reading poetry and playing snooker. 'I once took on the whole crew of My Left Foot. I played pool against seventeen of them and beat them all,' she recalls with satisfaction.

She plans never to diet or to remarry. 'The only thing you need men for is sex and to carry the bags,' she jokes. But she hasn't ruled out a return visit to Holby. 'I had hoped to make a guest appearance last year. But we couldn't get the script right. But who knows, next time..?'

CLIVE KING
State Registered Nurse Clive was second only to Charlie in the chain of command when we first went to Holby. Jamaican-born, he tolerated racist remarks, only occasionally letting his anger fly. Married with two small boys, he had been a gym teacher, still trained the local boys' football team and was often the department's best bet for turfing out troublemakers. Charming with children, his approach was relaxed but he was racked with stress because his low wage paid too few bills. As a result he smoked heavily and kept booze in his locker. Only Megan's beady eye and sharp tongue saved him from risking his job. Ewart talked the matter over with him. As an alcoholic himself, he understood.

George Harris

George Harris was already a well-known face when he played Holby's handsome hunk of a nurse. Probably Britain's best known black actor at the time, he'd had wide experience in theatre, film and television, including *Raiders of the Lost Ark* and the title roles of *Mandela* and *Wolcot* on television. In 1992 George partnered Doña Croll (who plays Adele Beckford in series eight) in the award-winning *Halleluyah Anyhow* and appeared in *Prime Suspect 2* and *Between the Lines*. He says he didn't feel that close to Clive, the drunk. 'I drink only purified water, I don't smoke and I'm a vegetarian.' He also prefers natural herbal remedies to orthodox medicine.

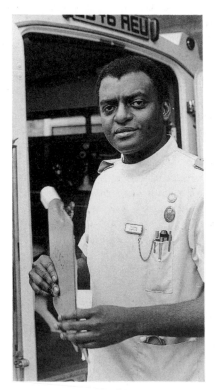

The Doctors

Mr MIKE BARRATT

He's a big man in a big job. As the A & E department's Consultant he's everything his predecessor Julian Chapman was not: friendly, well adjusted, able to understand and get on with ordinary people because he's one of them. Mike knows what it's like to make mistakes, he's made a few himself. The first was messing around at comprehensive school and failing to get the right A levels. The second was maybe to marry the wrong woman. Not that he's unhappy exactly with the as-yet-unseen Frances, who is older than him and has two teenage children. She's kept busy running an antiques stall at local craft fairs. It's just that there's often little of her time left for him. He does like women's company, you see. He likes Duffy, Adele, Helen, even headstrong Dr Karen Goodliffe. And he likes children, as is obvious when they come in for treatment. His large Mickey Mouse and King Kong ties are a great help there.

The young Mike re-sat and passed his A levels, then travelled the world while deciding what he'd like to do with his life. He scraped through to medical school but had to slog to keep up. But while he won't win a Nobel Prize for science his popularity has led to promotion. Patients can talk to him. Charlie and the team can work with him. Only Mark Calder, the new Surgical Manager, can't get what he wants from Big Mike because Mike doesn't give in easily when he's fighting to prevent cut-backs to the staff and equipment so badly needed by the department. And he has a giant-sized temper. Like Calder, Mike Barratt is a realist. He never believed that Holby becoming a Trust would be the Health Service's panacea. But like Julian, Mike Barratt is a doctor, not an actuary. Unlike Julian, he may tell Calder exactly where to stick his balance sheet.

Clive Mantle

Clive Mantle is as relaxed as his character Mike Barratt. He relishes the prospect of Mike's future challenges, especially the battles with meanie Mark Calder. As the only actor to have played opposite Clint Eastwood, beaten him up and LIVED, he feels fairly confident. His screen survival – unique in the Hollywood star's tough-guy films – came immediately before the 6ft 5½ in. tall Clive began at Holby last year. 'I had a small role in *White Hunter Black Heart* out in Africa with Clint Eastwood,' says Clive, who admits he's star-struck. 'When my teeth stopped chattering, it was great fun. Apparently it's the first time a Clint Eastwood character didn't get his own back.'

Clive, who lives in Wiltshire with his wife Zoe, grew up watching his cousin, actor John Hallam, in television roles and by the time he was in his teens he knew he wanted to follow him. He joined the National Youth Theatre, then went to RADA and has rarely been out of film, television, radio or stage work since. 'I spent twelve years on TV hitting people or

laughs. 'I'm used to all that. It's being recognized in a supermarket and asked when Julian's coming back that I can't bear!'

Dr KAREN GOODLIFFE

Hair scragged back, a frown fixed above her dark, worried eyes, the Senior House Officer looks as though she could do with a *Woman's Own* make-over, a large gin and tonic and more than just one good night's sleep. Even then she still wouldn't win any prizes for diplomacy and will still put her Dr Marten-clad foot in most conversations with Mark Calder or the visiting locum consultant, Mr Gordon. It's as though she thinks not being rude is sucking up. But 1993 *Casualty* watchers will soon learn that Dr Karen cares about the people who need caring about.

Unlike Rob Khalefa, Karen was not born to make life and death decisions for other people. Her mother was a mouse, her father a domineering dock workers' union rep who left their East London home when she was young. It turned her into a fighter and she's determined not to fail. She may go into psychological medicine or paediatrics. With luck by then she'll have prescribed herself some occasional fun too.

Suzanna Hamilton

Dark-haired Suzanna Hamilton has been inspired watching real doctors at Homerton Hospital in preparation for her role as *Casualty's* new SHO. 'I would like to have trained to be a doctor,' she says. 'It's a completely different way of

getting hit,' says the mild-mannered actor. Long stretches were spent making twenty-six episodes of *Robin of Sherwood* as (who else?) Little John. The punch-ups were often comic ones in *Smith and Jones*, *One Foot in the Grave*, *Jasper Carrott* and *The Lenny Henry Show*. He appeared in *Alien 3* and should have featured in *Superman 4* but the three months of work he spent on it

ended up on the cutting room floor.

He thinks he won the *Casualty* part because he could look jolly. The white coat is a touch short and he has to stoop now and then in a scene. 'I'm so much taller than the others that when I stand the camera has to shoot up. They find they have to change the lights and stick in extra bits of scenery,' he

life from mine. I found I wasn't squeamish as I watched operations. It was fascinating.'

Suzanna attended the Anna Scher Stage School. She appeared in several television dramas as a child, including the BBC's adaptation of *Swallows and Amazons*. She went on to the Central School of Drama and has worked steadily in films, including *Out of Africa* and *1984*, and on television, notably as one of the wartime heroines in the LWT serial *Wish Me Luck*. She has played a doctor only once before, a glamorous one in the Central series *Tecx*. For Dr Karen she was warned that there wouldn't be a penny spent on her costume or make-up. 'I thought at first that that would be a relief,' she said. 'But starting work at 8.30 a.m. some days, looking like death, I could do with make-up – the works.'

Dr ANDREW BOWER

Andrew Bower was the Medical Registrar who helped Dr Lucy, as well as the Holby team, in 1989.

Not too sympathetic a character then, he only seemed interested in his own career.

His relationship with Duffy seemed to be one of convenience for him. When she became pregnant he expected her to sacrifice her career for his and they parted acrimoniously and contact ceased. But when Duffy had a cancer scare in 1992 she began to worry that her small son might need his other parent, so she contacted Andrew and sent him photographs of the child. By coincidence he was shortly to return to Holby as the locum consultant, taking over when Julian abruptly left. Andrew came back as handsome as ever, but he was more mature, more worthy of our favourite Sister. He was also shown to like children, smiling warmly when young Peter

burst into the department, beaming with delight to learn that this was his son. He lost out to Mike Barratt for the permanent job. But he made things permanent with Duffy at the end of the seventh series. They may even try for a second child.

William Gaminara

His mother and sister are both doctors but actor and playwright William Gaminara never wanted to set foot inside a hospital. Unfortunately, just before he returned to Holby last year, he was unable to work for six months thanks to a slipped disc caused by a wrong move in a squash game. During that time he spent three tedious weeks strapped to a hospital bed undergoing traction. When he arrived at the warehouse where some of *Casualty* is filmed he had another, less serious injury – a burned hand. 'It was just something from the kitchen but the burn had developed into violent colours. The make-up people there fell on me, they love to study these things. They pinned my hand to a table and took notes!'

Londoner William is married to actress Kate Lock and they have two small sons, Joe and Fred. His play *Back up the Hearse and Let Them Sniff the Flowers* was performed at the Hampstead Theatre last year. And he is now a regular on *The Archers* BBC radio serial, playing another doctor, the eligible Richard Locke. 'Luckily, whenever I need to, I can telephone my sister to find out how to pronounce the medical terms.'

Dr ROBERT KHALEFA

Rob Khalefa was certainly the pin-up of Holby's A & E in 1992. The looks were more impressive than the skills at first, though. Rob the doctor was arrogant, careless, panicky under pressure and unwilling to take advice from more experienced staff. Rob the colleague was a disaster as Sandra Nicholl discovered when he allowed her to take the rap for a mistake he forced on to her.

A second generation Iranian, his father had been a brilliant surgeon and there was pressure on him to follow in the same footsteps. But if his connections had opened doors for him, they hardly impressed Charlie and Duffy, to whom he was rude and dismissive. Nor was Julian Chapman impressed when he checked some X-rays and saw what Rob had missed.

Over the weeks we saw him suffer doubts that he could do the job and, the more he doubted, the better he became. He had a girlfriend but he almost let her drown when they went boating together. At Holby his only friend seemed to be Maxine, the chirpy Health Care Assistant. But by the time rioters were burning down the hospital he was one of the 'family'. Risking his life to rescue an already dead patient, he was engulfed by the flames. His survival seemed impossible. Yet as the new series starts, Norma the receptionist mentions him. He's in hospital and recovering. Those chiselled looks may have changed. But should he pick up the stethoscope again, he's sure to be the best doctor in Britain.

Jason Riddington

During his drama school training Jason Riddington was always being cast as fat drunken old men. But the day he arrived in Holby, teenage girls tore down rock stars' posters from their bedroom walls

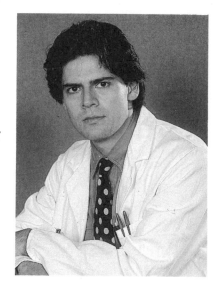

and stopped sending love letters to Todd in *Neighbours*. Did they mind that you wouldn't trust him to dab calamine lotion on a gnat bite? Of course not. Sadly, handsome, friendly Jason has eyes only for his new daughter, the child he and actress Claire Laurie produced early in 1993. Claire, a student at the Bristol Old Vic theatre company, met Jason when she worked as an extra playing a relief nurse on *Casualty* and the diagnosis was love.

In all it has been an eventful few years for the Derby-born actor who had seemed set to become a tennis star until an injury ended his hopes. He left school early, much to his teachers' relief, he

jokes. A leading role in *The Beggar's Opera* in Coventry followed drama school, then came the role of Hareton, the gentle brute, in the film of *Wuthering Heights*. Since leaving *Casualty* he has filmed episodes of two new dramas for television, *Highlander* and *Berlin Breaks*, and starred in the stage play *Salsa Celestina* with Paul Medford. No doubt he has also made several appearances at Mothercare.

Mr JULIAN CHAPMAN

When he arrived at Holby in 1990, Dr (as he was then) Chapman was an upper class, medical version of Victor Meldrew, a man in a permanent state of exasperation and pessimism who, one felt, smiled only at coronations to please the servants. He and his patients seemed to come from different worlds.

Beth and Charlie suffered the worst of his impatience and were most shocked by his doomy dismissal of patients' problems. The trouble was he was often right – they couldn't change things. His doctoring was never less than efficient, his surgical skills were often awe-inspiring. We saw nothing of his home life and learned only from the briefest remarks that he had two failed marriages behind him, that alcohol had been a problem at one stage and he'd been a heavy smoker. Also, he knew the correct pronunciation of a patient's African name, suggesting that there had been a colonial childhood. Perhaps that was when he saw his brother die? Perhaps that was why shooting paint pellets at his yuppie chums in war games was a fitting weekend sport for him? The fighting spirit showed when the job of Consultant came up. He put his mind to the task, used the old boy network, and Andrew Bower and the other applicants stood little chance. Mr (no longer Dr) Chapman seemed set up, settled. He wasn't, of course.

Thanks to Nigel Le Vaillant, the actor who played him, Julian thawed and developed into a believable human being in his three years at Holby. More than that, he became a heart-throb for female viewers of all ages and his pigeonhole at the warehouse was always crammed with fan letters from women wanting to play doctors and nurses with him.

Julian's hesitant but then headlong affair with Sandra Nicholl was perhaps THE hospital romance *Casualty* fans had waited seven years to enjoy. When the Scottish Staff Nurse turned up at his flat at the end of her shift and announced that she didn't know about him but she was going to bed, swooning swept across the land. Eat your heart out, Mills and Boon. She didn't need a stethoscope to detect a decent manly heart beating underneath his Simpsons' shirts and old school tie. Her small daughter, Laura, found a man who could play with dolls. Who was surprised? Only Julian. The love affair was never as secret as he thought. And it was no secret at all after he accompanied an injured trapeze artist back to

Holby – he'd been at the circus with Laura.

Anyway, he was free. Ironically, he was also free to care more about his patients and Holby City Hospital than he had ever cared before. That's what led to his angry decision to quit, when the hospital said there was no money to buy a vital piece of equipment for patients with spinal injuries but it could find enough cash to redecorate the board room. He argued furiously with Simon Eastman, the administrator, spoke to the press about the cash shortages and then jumped in his Mercedes and zoomed out of Holby.

> # I saw Julian as a lonely, isolated man, emotionally a mess. The reason he was so angry all the time was that it masked his shyness.

Would Sandra agree to leave her husband for him? We half hoped she would but guessed she wouldn't. Well, not immediately. As with all good soap stories, their relationship continues off-screen. We think of them together eventually. They were meant to be.

Nigel Le Vaillant

Nigel Le Vaillant has more than his fair-haired good looks in common with Julian Chapman, the tetchy doctor he played for fifty episodes until series seven. They share similar backgrounds. The actor was born and grew up in Pakistan, where his father was chairman of Brooke Bond Tea. He went to a public school. He proved brainy, reading English at Oxford, and was single-minded about pursuing his chosen career despite the hardships. He joined Birmingham Rep, then the Royal Shakespeare Company. 'Then things fell apart for a few years, once or twice I thought I'd never work again,' he says candidly. A stint at the National Theatre, television roles in such series as *Jemima Shore Investigates*, and *A Question of Guilt* and parts in films such as *Personal Services* followed, but did not prevent him being out of work for fourteen months before the *Casualty* role came up. Like Julian, Nigel can seem distant. 'I suppose we are both intense,' he admits. 'I saw Julian as a lonely, isolated man, emotionally a mess. The reason he was so angry all the time was that it masked his shyness. And people shied away from him because of his manner.'

On the other hand, Nigel is certainly no 'man apart'. While filming the 1990 series he shared a Bristol flat with Patrick Robinson, who plays Ash, and Robson Green, who played Jimmy. He struck up an easy friendship with Nicola Jeffries as soon as she joined the cast in 1991 to play the assistant receptionist, and they soon became

'I hated the scene where I had to amputate a boy's foot, even though I knew it was a lump of wood. When I had to put my hand in a gaping hole in a man's chest to pull a cross bow bolt out – squeeze his liver with one hand as I pulled the thing out with the other – I really thought I was going to faint. I had a bunch of make-up people behind me saying, "Don't be so pathetic, it's just a bit of latex." I can say for sure that I picked up no medical knowledge whatsoever in my three years in Holby. I could never, ever, have studied medicine. But I have friends who did and are now doctors. They didn't pull my leg – they just seemed very jealous that I was promoted to consultant before they were!" he laughs.

Nigel was delighted with the Julian and Sandra storyline. 'She was just the sort of woman who would get through to him, someone from a completely different social background. She cut straight through all of that.'

Nigel decided to leave when he felt the role was no longer a challenge. He said he didn't want to become a long-running character like *Coronation Street*'s Ken Barlow. He hopes in future to explore comedy parts. But in his first post-Holby job he was strapped to a bed, the 'patient' of a mad woman in the stage version of Stephen King's horror story *Misery*.

Dr BETH RAMANEE
Probably the best-loved woman doctor ever to pull back a Holby cubicle curtain, Beth Ramanee replaced Lucy as the SHO. Her

a couple. Unlike Julian with Sandra. 'When he started to fall in love he was embarrassed and rather shifty about the whole thing, he didn't want to give way to his feelings,' laughed Nigel.

Most importantly the actor couldn't have worked among the wounded like Julian. It was a standing joke on the set that while the character was so unflinching dealing with the horrific injuries of his patients, Nigel turned green around the gills just fumbling with fake flesh. He would never have watched himself as Julian on television. 'I can remember being at home flicking through the channels on TV and there was a heart operation. My girlfriend carried on eating a hamburger but I had to leave the room.

three, at first. (Nigel Le Vaillant, who played him, actually urged the writers to allow Julian's attitude to change so that he could have a fling with her, but it wasn't to be.)

We learned almost nothing about Beth's private life, she seemed to have no time for one. The most stressful period for her was after she chose to respect a dying patient's wishes not to be resuscitated. It led to the patient's daughter accusing her of negligence. Beth was eventually cleared but shaken. She left Holby to work as a GP after demonstrating patience above and beyond the call of duty. At her interview she was asked when she intended to return to 'her own country'. It seems Beth still has many battles to fight.

Mamta Kaash

Slim, quietly spoken Mamta Kaash came to Britain from India at the age of eleven and developed an interest in acting when she was at school in London. She played nurses in *Emmerdale* and *Angels* before taking the role of a Moslem girl in love with a Jewish boy in BBC TV's *Shalom Salaam*, for which she won the Best Actress prize at the Cannes Television Festival. She was immediately offered a film role but when it fell through she was able to say 'yes' to the offer from *Casualty* three days before rehearsals started. After two years she decided people were beginning to think she was a doctor rather than an actress, 'although I can't tell a leg from a liver' she jokes. 'I'm also very squeamish. When my sister had a

parents were Indian, but she'd never been to India. She'd grown up in Cheltenham but hadn't had a silver-spoon education at the Ladies' College. Instead, she had attended a sixth form college and, with both feet on the ground, had slogged through medical school. It had made her a compassionate doctor, with a social conscience, one who wanted genuinely to help a drug addict or a prostitute

suffering from hepatitis by admitting them to hospital. When she tried to do this, her superior Julian Chapman slapped her down for becoming too involved. His attitude was patch 'em up and pass 'em on. Beth's diagnostic and clinical skills soon impressed her colleagues and she even earned the respect of Julian, who had put her down on snobbish, sexist or racist grounds, or perhaps all

nose bleed once, I was shaken up, I ended up in hospital. Even when I had to give injections into false skin in *Casualty* if you looked hard you could see my hand trembling.'

She also learned that it sometimes doesn't pay to tell your director too much. When filming a scene in which a patient was going to vomit blood all over Dr Beth, Mamta mentioned that she had brought a couple of blouses with her. 'He made us do the scene three times. I was absolutely soaked in so-called blood,' she said. Since leaving the series, the 30-year-old actress has attended RADA 'to relearn the classics'. She has appeared on the stage and in several TV dramas including *Between the Lines*, and in the summer of 1993 appeared in her first singing and dancing role in the stage play *Moti Roti Batli Chunni*. She looks back on *Casualty* fondly. While Beth and Julian fought on screen, she and Nigel Le Vaillant used to reminisce about the similar lands where they grew up. 'Nigel used to practise his Urdu on me and suggest we run away together,' she laughed.

Dr LUCY PERRY

Middle class, liberated and lovely (despite never having time to fix her long dark hair or put on make-up), Lucy learned a lot during her stint at Holby. On her first day in September 1989 as Casualty Officer she was thrown in at the deep end, having to operate on a crash victim on the road. It showed her colleagues that whatever else, she knew her medicine and didn't mind getting her hands dirty.

Like Baz, the bedside manner was soothing. Lucy could also be tough. But, unlike Baz, she wasn't used to battling with a slow and often illogical hospital system where 'urgent' often meant 'when it suits'. She argued with Charlie and with administrator Valerie, and hated to kowtow to consultants. Skilful with her hands, Lucy already knew she wanted to progress to general surgery and asked Dr Andrew Bower to help. Perhaps she harboured a tiny longing for him which may have affected her attitude to Duffy, whom she once described as 'a bit of a schoolma'am'. Certainly Lucy was a new thinker, an art lover, a believer in holistic approaches, full of surprises. Alternatively, she was, as one of her patients concluded, 'an oddball'. But a most attractive one.

Tam Hoskyns

During her stint as a spectator at a London hospital while researching her role as Dr Lucy Perry, Tam Hoskyns was mistaken for a real doctor. It was a stunning experience. A nurse asked her to take over trying to resuscitate a man who had attempted suicide. 'The blood rushed to my feet. I looked blank but I did all I could.' Sadly the man died. 'It was the first time I'd seen a dead body and I was still thinking about it when I drove to the theatre later. I was involved in a collision, both cars were written off. Fortunately, no one was hurt but I'm lucky to be alive. It made me realise the fine line between life and death.'

Tam, daughter of business expert and government policy advisor Sir John Hoskyns, had left RADA three years earlier after university and had worked with Kenneth Branagh's Renaissance Theatre Company between trekking around the world and doing the occasional bit of busking. Since *Casualty* she has appeared on television in *The Naked Actor* and worked with Alan Ayckbourn in Scarborough. Given the choice, Tam would prefer to be a writer than an actress. She has already written a series of plays.

Dr DAVID ROWE

As a medical student, David Rowe might have had hearty nights on the town with Rob Khalefa, who had the same job at Holby a few years after David left. They were

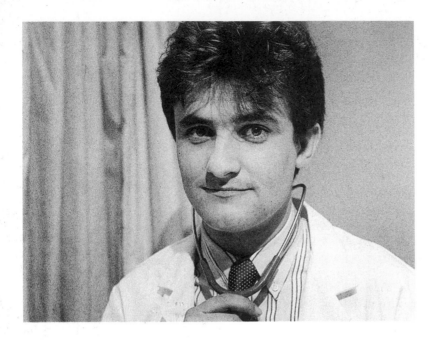

two of a kind, both public school-educated boys with good intentions, good brains and an almost criminal ignorance of how most people lived. Actor Paul Lacoux, who played him, summed David up as 'a plonker'. But where Rob was arrogant, David was naive and visibly upset when he was unable to help seriously injured patients, such as the young girl who was paralysed while working in a garage. He was daunted when he had to talk to grief-stricken relatives. Luckily there were more experienced doctors, Ewart and Peter, and the Medical Registrar (Brian Capron) to whom he could turn for advice. In his favour, David was kind to children, sensitive with young women and, after he first exploded at Charlie and Cyril for playing with his hockey sticks, he loosened up and challenged them to a game.

Paul Lacoux

One of Paul Lacoux's brothers is a doctor and his sister is a nurse. But the handsome dark-haired Londoner says he had to become an actor – with only one O level, he hadn't the brains to do anything else! His hospital research for the part of Dr David Rowe was a baptism of fire. 'I was there when a house burned down with seven dossers in it. One of them was badly burned and he tried to get off the table while he was being treated. They asked me to help hold him down. It didn't disturb me too much. But in one of our scenes I had to put someone's shoulder back into place. When I saw it on the screen they had added the sound effects and you could hear the crunch. I thought "Oh God!"'

Paul trained at the Bristol Old Vic Theatre School and his television credits include roles in *Fortunes of War*, *The Singing Detective* (he played a doctor in the famous 'Dem Dry Bones' scene), *Sherlock Holmes* and *Poirot*. But in the nine months before the call to *Casualty* came he'd worked only in two fringe theatre shows and earned nothing. Dr David, 'plonker' or not, was a hero to Paul's bank manager. His latest roles have seen him on stage at the Liverpool Everyman and in the West End in *Gift of the Gorgon*.

Dr MARY TOMLINSON

So-serious Mary Tomlinson was the first of a line of unworldly young doctors who were 'broken in' by the nurses of Holby. Duffy called her 'po-faced' and Megan likened her to Dr Zhivago when she handed out a list of jobs. Her allegedly boring boyfriend, Brendan (Jonathan Oliver), was gossiped about and Cyril bet Charlie he could get her to go out with him, nudge nudge. He succeeded, but Mary had guessed what was happening and turned what should have been a cheap after-shift breakfast rendezvous into a lavish meal at an expensive hotel. She earned Duffy's trust when she was able to advise her on taking an HIV test and gradually we saw that Mary could smile too.

Mary had been working at St Stephen's and approached Ewart at the celebrations that followed winning back the night shift, telling him how much she admired his stand against the management. She asked to take over Baz's post of SHO in 1987.

Above: Megan may be only a State Enrolled Nurse but she can take Charlie down a peg or two

Left: Ewart fails to cure Kuba of the porter's patients' flower fetish

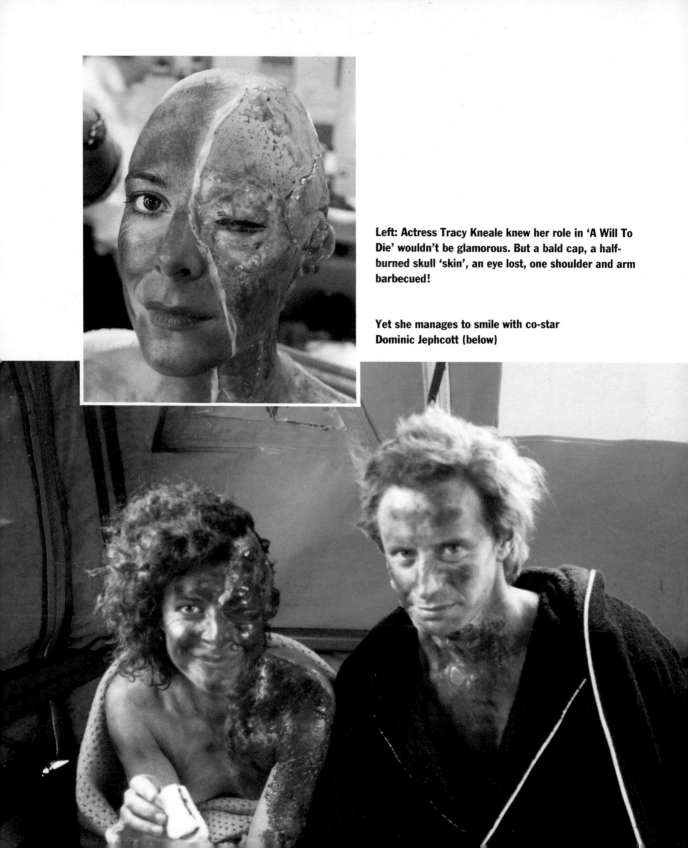

Left: Actress Tracy Kneale knew her role in 'A Will To Die' wouldn't be glamorous. But a bald cap, a half-burned skull 'skin', an eye lost, one shoulder and arm barbecued!

Yet she manages to smile with co-star Dominic Jephcott (below)

Left: *Casualty's* first illicit lovers, Andy (Robert Pugh) and Sandra (Lisa Bowerman) seldom looked cheerful

Below: Julian's other job turned out to be 'soldiering' for fun, shooting paint pellets at pals in the woods

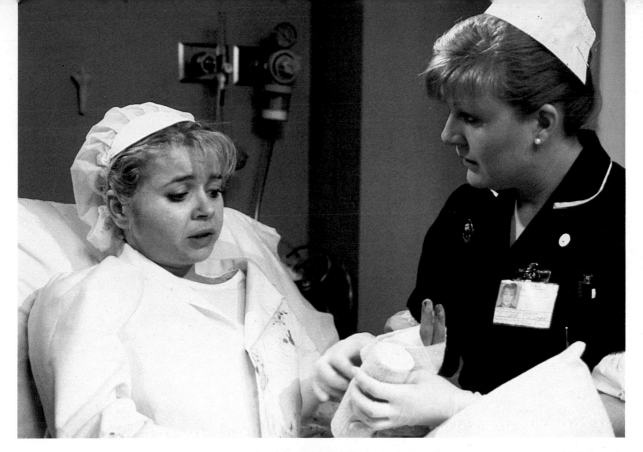

Above: A bride-to-be (Ingrid Lacey) hopes to make it to the church with her chopped off finger back in place

Right: It's all over, said a bedraggled Duffy as flames engulfed the department. 'Nonsense, woman, pull yourself together!' we replied

Left: Young female viewers swooned when Dr Rob Khalefa (Jason Riddington) joined in 1992. Thank goodness Charlie and Duffy were there to spot some of the mistakes

Above left: My, how Duffy's boy Peter has grown!

Above right: Does Dr Andrew Bower (William Gaminara) deserve Duffy's hand?

Right: Happier days for Martin Ashford (Patrick Robinson) and his student girlfriend Nikki (Imogen Boorman)

Left: Some day, somewhere, Sandra (Maureen Beattie) and Julian (Nigel Le Vaillant) will be together

Back in the swing! Charlie, Dr Mike Barratt (Clive Mantle) and his team for 1993

All-too-conscious that she came from a humble home in Walker, Newcastle upon Tyne, Mary had taken elocution lessons to lose her Geordie accent. Her parents doted on her and were proud as punch of her achievements but the relationship was now strained. When they visited her at Holby and Dad (Bryan Pringle) was taken ill, Ewart had to treat him because Mary was too embarrassed. She left Holby to go into general surgery.

Helena Little

Having grown up in Africa, Helena Little speaks fluent Swahili. She trained at the Guildhall School of Music and Drama in London and worked steadily through the 1980s on stage and in television. After leaving *Casualty* at the end of the second series Helena appeared in ITV's *Capital City*, the BBC series

Waterfront Beat, the serial *Children of the North*, played in *Dancing at Lughansa* on the West End stage and produced and starred in a two-hander, *Danny and the Deep Blue Sea*. She recently became a mother.

EWART PLIMMER

Casualty's first Clinical Assistant was Ewart Plimmer. Wise, Welsh and no longer young, by that stage in his career he was a 'hands-off' physician, who rarely put his white coat on over his sports jacket and dealt with patients only when forced. He was, however, a passionate supporter of his department and a good friend to his staff. He talked to them as equals but he could be stern: the white moustache could bristle, the bushy eyebrows knit together.

As he sat in his grim office, plugged into his Walkman, we saw in him the loneliness of the long shifts' doctor. His home life had crumbled because he worked at night. His wife Roz threw him out and his eighteen-year-old daughter Gillian disappeared. No wonder he drank. When, in the second year, he had won his battle for the night shift, there was time for love. Administrator Elizabeth Straker was ideal for him, although they argued almost constantly. But happiness eluded him. Worried about a new threat to his observation ward, he suffered a seizure, then a heart attack, which proved fatal.

Bernard Gallagher

Born and brought up in Bradford, Bernard Gallagher has worked at

the Royal Court, the Old Vic and the National Theatre and has completed a season with the Royal Shakespeare Company. In 1993 he worked in *Getting Married* on stage at Chichester.

His face is well known from countless appearances on television as a lawyer, teacher and journalist. Ewart was Bernard's first and only doctor, though. 'I was in two minds when I learned Ewart was going to be killed off,' he says. 'I was happy with the programme but I was also happy to go because it meant I could go back to the theatre.' Since leaving *Casualty*, he has appeared in other television shows including *The Bill*, *The Harry Enfield Show* and *This is David Lander*.

Dr BARBARA SAMUELS

Affectionately known as Baz, Dr Barbara Samuels was *Casualty's* Senior House Officer when Holby's doors were first opened to us. She was an excellent doctor and a liberated woman who didn't wilt when macho patients demanded to see a 'proper' doctor, meaning a man. But she knew she wanted something else, something better. The problem was what? She no longer wanted to work in A & E. Ewart had persuaded her to stay on after her first six months there but she felt the strain.

Baz seemed to live well enough, in a comfortable flat, with good clothes and a racy car that she enjoyed driving fast. To ward off the tiredness she sometimes took amphetamines which made Charlie cross. But she humoured him. At twenty-eight she was uninhibited about sex and enjoyed Charlie's company, among others', in bed. But while Baz liked babies and was kind to pregnant patients, she didn't hesitate to have a termination when she became pregnant herself. Taking a few days off work, she called in with 'a cold', but she'd been spotted at an abortion clinic with a male friend. Baz denied what she'd done when Kuba, the porter, innocently asked. Only to Charlie did Baz tell the truth. He was hurt – it had been his child. After this, she left, and this time she didn't tell Charlie. He rang around searching for her. Only later did he receive her letter saying she'd found a job in London.

Julia Watson

When pretty dark-haired Julia Watson put on a white coat to

observe what really happens in operating theatres before playing Baz, she found herself watching a foot coming off and felt her knees going weak. Although she doubts whether she could have become a doctor, she approved of Baz and was surprised that her behaviour was seen by some as shocking. 'Why shouldn't women doctors go out with male nurses?' she asks.

Having left the show after the first year, Julia married poet David Harsent and they have a young daughter, Hannah. She has worked in several BBC dramas, including *A Touch of Spice*, and starred in the ITV movie, *To Each His Own*, along with Robert Pugh who played surly ambulance man Andrew Ponting. She will be seen in *Lovejoy* in 1994.

The Paramedics

JOSH GRIFFITHS

The smiling intelligent face of paramedic Josh is the one you'd want to see if you'd fallen out of the bathroom window in the altogether. That's why he has been a favourite with viewers, epecially young ones, since he arrived in 1990. But often he can't joke about what he meets when he gets a call. He's the first one to see the mangled bodies and deal with the hysterical victims and their distraught relatives. Josh doesn't show it, but he feels things deeply. He's devoted to his wife, Helen, and their two children, one of whom was born with cystic fibrosis and is now wheelchair-bound. His friendship with Jane, his ambulance driving partner, is also profound, so much so that Helen has often felt jealous of what they share. She doesn't know what it is – partly because Josh doesn't tell her about the times when he has been threatened, hit or half-strangled by deranged people. Highly trained, his quick thinking has saved countless lives. Off-duty, he likes to potter, do DIY, help the local youth football team train. It takes his mind off the waste of life he might witness tomorrow.

Ian Bleasdale

Former teacher Ian Bleasdale regularly joins professional ambulance crews on shifts and, with his screen partner Jane, played by Caroline Webster, is guided in every action scene by Clive Haddrell or a colleague from the Avon Ambulance Service.

'I certainly couldn't do it for real. Playing Josh has given me confidence that I could cope with the first aid, the "there, there's", even the overdoses, strokes and falls. But dealing with the relatives is just too tough,' he says. He must act convincingly though, because, like most of the *Casualty* cast, Ian finds that strangers expect him to know what to do in emergencies. Even his wife, Andie, a school's deputy head, sometimes forgets his is an acting job.

'She hurt her toe last year and expected me to know what to do. She was cross when I said "go to the hospital", and when she did and found it was broken she accused me of wrongly diagnosing it!' he laughs.

Lancashire born Ian, who now lives in Howarth and has a small son, jokes that his mother took to her bed when he decided to chuck in his safe job of teaching to go to the Everyman Theatre, Liverpool. 'She was right,' he says. 'I've

staggered from unemployment to unemployment.' In between he has appeared as an Aids sufferer in *Brookside*, as a glum shepherd in *All Creatures Great and Small* and in *Coronation Street* as a photographer who got tough with Mike Baldwin. 'I love playing Josh, especially now that he is to join a special front line team. He'll be driving a motorbike and travelling by helicopter.' Ian is learning to fly helicopters as a hobby, so he has been lobbying the writers to let Josh learn too.

JANE SCOTT

Pretty divorcée Jane Scott, Josh's paramedic partner, is an action woman. She drives, she dashes, she climbs into buildings, she abseils down cliffs. She uses karate on troublemakers and keeps her customers alive with her cheerful chat. She even looks good in her baggy green dungarees. Or at least, she did do all those things. But nothing lasts forever and Jane, educated and thinking of her future, has decided to go on a management course in series eight. She succeeds, of course, and becomes the Associate General Manager of A & E. A satisfying switch? Caroline Webster, who plays her, will say only, 'We'll see a new side of her character. And we'll see what she looks like in real clothes. She'll have to live up to her shoulder pads.'

Caroline Webster

Caroline Webster first played Jane in one episode of the 1990 series – Jane was spattered with blood and Jimmy the porter made a pass at her. Despite that, when she was invited back the fair-haired actress from Kent jumped at the chance to continue playing the feisty, forthright paramedic. Like Ian Bleasdale, who plays her fellow paramedic, Josh, Caroline went out with a real ambulance crew and was present when they found an elderly man dead. 'I'd never seen a corpse before and though it may sound ghoulish, it was quite liberating. But I'm sure I couldn't take the constant pressure paramedics work under.'

Caroline has worked mainly in the theatre since leaving drama school. She spent a couple of happy years with Alan Ayckbourn's company in Scarborough and toured the Middle East with Derek Nimmo's. She appeared in other uniforms in *The Bill* and *London's Burning* on television before putting on her *Casualty* jumpsuits. Two things tickle her about playing Jane. 'The specification for the role was that Jane was "buxom" and I'm certainly not that. And no one ever asked me if I could drive. Luckily for the ambulances, I can.'

The Receptionists

NORMA SULLIVAN

When she first made a stately appearance behind the desk in the A & E reception in 1991, Norma Sullivan showed she had standards. Married with grown-up sons, she hid the fact that she also cared for a mother with Alzheimer's disease. She seemed stiff and stuffy, as though she deserved a grander job than that of a receptionist. Julian Chapman's personal secretary, perhaps? At least he was a gentleman, not like some of them she had to deal with. Couldn't even keep a civil tongue. Couldn't tell you clearly their names and addresses! Really!

Anne Kristen, who has played her so convincingly, believes Norma's crossness was a cover-up for her inefficiency. 'She did several frightful things, including sending away a body builder who had diabetes. She told him to go to his own doctor,' she recalls. In the new series Norma is again tetchy but this time it's a symptom of a difficult menopause. Her colleagues don't spot it. It occurs to Charlie that she may be drinking and Mark Calder prepares to make another staff cut.

Anne Kristen

Some of the angry letters she received told Anne Kristen that her character Norma has upset some hospital workers. So when she fell over in the street and hurt her hand in early 1993 Anne was nervous at the thought of having it

X-rayed. Sure enough, when she arrived at the desk of the BRI's A & E ward, a woman said frostily, 'You're talking to a real receptionist now!' Anne, from Glasgow, based her playing of Norma on a surgery dragon she knew from way back but hopes the human side of her character has been obvious too.

Now in her fifties, Anne knew she wanted to be an actress from the time she appeared in a primary school nativity play. 'I remember declaring "I am the black king Melkiar!" and I loved it.' After Scottish RADA she joined the Citizens' Theatre and has played most of the great classic roles in her time. She has made countless television appearances, notably as a murderess in *Taggart* and a snotty Englishwoman in *Rab C Nesbit*.

For the new series divorcée Anne is happy to play a woman going through the physical and psychological problems of the menopause. 'I've done it all. For me it was a piece of cake but I know the mood swings and dizziness are awful for some women and it's not a subject that's often discussed openly. I'm looking forward to becoming sixty, getting a bus pass and going on Saga holidays.'

MIE NISHI-KAWA
Mie has moved from the admin department, where she was a clerk-typist, to the A & E reception. She's only twenty-two but she knows her own mind.

When her Japanese parents returned home after living in the USA and London she refused to join them, worried about the hostility of some Japanese towards those who return with Western attitudes. So she is staying with an uncle who runs a car factory in Holby.

Naoko Mori
There are more than a few parallels between Naoko's background and her character's – Naoko's father is an international businessman. Because of his work, the family moved first to America and then came to Britain in 1984. She enjoyed acting and singing at school, and was planning to go to drama school when an understudy part in the West End musical *Miss Saigon* came along. Naoko won the job and stayed in the show for three years, often taking the main female role. In that time she also appeared in the television comedies *Absolutely Fabulous* and *Desmond's*. 'My family are back in Japan now but I chose not to go. I feel I'm a fairly liberated woman, I don't know how I'd fit into the Japanese culture now.' Naoko was thrilled when the role of Mie was created. 'The only thing is that I love singing. But you can't have a singing receptionist in a casualty department, I suppose.'

SUSIE MERCIER
Slightly-built young Susie, the first *Casualty* receptionist, was a one-woman peace corps. She could charm angry policemen, defuse and calm fighting drunks, and flatter local bigwigs. Efficient and cheerful with patients, snappily dressed and coiffed, Susie was also Holby's best gossip. When she left after two series, Holby lost a treasure.

Debbie Roza
Petite Asian actress Debbie Roza has worked for the Polka

Children's Theatre and Foco Novo and made a variety of television appearances including a part in Horace Ove's *Moving Portraits* and the lead in HTV's *The Function Room*. Since leaving *Casualty* she has left these shores to pursue her career in Canada.

Porters

FRANKIE DRUMMER
Got a nasty rash, a gyppy tummy, a bit of pain? Frankie Drummer, the new porter, can diagnose and cure you as he pushes your wheelchair up to the casualty reception desk. Or so he reckons.

Some people think Frankie's a bit of a pain himself. Others think he's a right laugh. He is certainly a comic character, all bluster and blubber. He has definite opinions on doctors, nurses, gay people ('backs to the wall, here comes another one') and what would 'put this country right'. If he doesn't say it, he pulls a face, rolls the eyes. You may disagree, but

he's harmless. When there's a rumpus in the department, he's worth his weight in gold. That's some weight. Viewers to series eight will see him having to get tough with trouble-makers soon enough.

Frankie, who's in his thirties, likes his grub and his home comforts. He had a well-paid job as a manual worker in a factory until the recession changed things and he and the wife decided to come back to Holby, her hometown. He thinks the world of her and his three kids. Pity they're all girls, he says. Nice to have a boy. Perhaps next time. No danger of his not settling down in the new job. Suits him down to the ground. Since he did that first aid course, there's not much old

Frankie can't tell you about health and the health service given half a chance.

Steven O'Donnell

Unlike his character Frankie, one thing actor Steven O'Donnell is not interested in is talking about the health service and illness non-stop. He spent five years trying to get out of a Charing Cross hospital, where he worked as a Junior Medical Laboratory Scientific Officer to become an actor.

'It's a real laugh that the best job I've had on television – this one – puts me right back in hospital!' says the 31-year-old Londoner. One lunchtime eight years ago, disillusioned with what he felt was his 'dogsbody' work in the lab, he was joking with colleagues in the canteen when a secretary said to him, 'You ought to leave.' 'I said, "Right, I will" and I gave in my letter of resignation that week. The poor girl became quite worried for me and my parents thought I was mad to give up a steady job.'

Steven had already appeared in a few youth theatre plays and began hunting for work in the Fringe theatres. He appeared on television in comedies such as *Bottom* and *The Comic Strip* and won good reviews for his playing of a brutal murderer in an ITV drama. 'A convincing slob' one critic wrote. He hoped Hollywood would become his next base after appearing as Tom Cruise's brother in the film *Far And Away*. 'I was sure the offers would flood in – but the phone never rang.'

Despite a few lean times, he never went hungry, luckily, because Steven has found he's in demand as a fattie. 'I'm more enormous than roly-poly,' he jokes. 'It's an asset. I don't know what a diet is – and I don't want to find out.'

JIMMY POWELL

Jaunty Jimmy was the addition to the 1989 team after Kuba left. From the hints given by the good-looking young Geordie, he'd had a chequered career up to then and it included a criminal record for theft. His three years at Holby were the longest he'd held down a job. But although he enjoyed

meeting people, chatting up numerous nurses and women patients, he was restless.

We learned that he often did a spot of moonlighting on a market stall, after a fire in the market brought him into A & E with a young girl patient. It was an important moment – the macho front cracked and he wasn't able to hide the tears. A lot of what Jimmy saw at Holby made him think he should change his life. He toyed with the idea of training to become a nurse but a lack of confidence mixed with a natural laziness made him drop the idea. Jimmy left Holby at the end of 1991 to drive a van for a friend in the rag trade. But he couldn't drive at that point – he asked the chaps in paramedics to give him a few lessons.

Robson Green

Natural comic Robson Green was an immediate hit as the cocky porter Jimmy. The ex-shipyard worker from Dudley, Northumberland, had acted at school and in youth theatre. In 1986 he gave up his job – by then he'd graduated to the design department at the shipyard – to take roles in Newcastle's Live Theatre. He was soon picked for television roles in BBC's *Hands* and then *Casualty*. 'When I saw my first few performances as Jimmy, I was horrified. There was this wooden, terrified guy.'

In 1991 we were also able to see Robson as accident-prone Corporal Tucker in ITV's *Soldier Soldier*. He also fitted stage work into his busy schedule, appearing as Jesus in a Mystery play. Robson decided to leave *Casualty* when he felt the role of Jimmy was no longer a challenge. He has since set up his own small television production company.

KUBA TRZCINSKI

Kuba, the Holby porter for the first three years, was Polish and spoke strangled, formal English with a strong accent. His haven was the porters' lodge where he hoarded 'borrowed' equipment from other wards, patients' flowers and the paraphernalia needed to make the special Polish tea which he sometimes offered his none-too-grateful colleagues. He liked to watch videos of the Royal Family, to dance, sing and rehearse little speeches to the various ladies he admired and sometimes shyly approached. Ewart had to reprimand him when he found he had been

taking hospital linen home. It was to help his landlady. It was easy to forgive him.

Chivalrous and old-fashioned, Kuba often seemed a purely comic character. But he was highly intelligent and sensitive and was the hero of the hour in the opening episode 'Gas', when he identified the toxic substance which was threatening the lives of dock workers.

Christopher Rozycki

A tall, dark-haired Polish actor with a broad smile, Christopher Rozycki changed his character's original nationality from Hungarian to match his own. But his creation incurred the wrath of some Polish viewers who thought the man was too much of a clown.

'I thought he was realistic. Like many Polish people in England for the first time he was naive, confused and trying to make a new life,' he says.

The actor graduated from the Lodz School of Theatre and Film in 1966 and spent thirteen years with the Stefan Jaracz Theatre Company in Poland. He worked for the Polish Theatre Company in London and appeared in a variety of television dramas, including the true spy story *Wynne and Penkovsky* in the role of Penkovsky. He also played Victor in the film *Local Hero* and, since leaving *Casualty*, has appeared in the BBC serial *Sleepers*, the comedy *Drop the Dead Donkey* and the award-winning film *Truly, Madly, Deeply*, in which he played a man not unlike Kuba, the neighbour who is in love with Juliet Stevenson's character.

We saw it as a horrific cycling accident. A bike pedal had ripped into a rider's abdomen and emergency surgery was needed to save his life.

In the Tytherleigh household they saw it as dad spending hours punching pubic hairs into a man's groin. Well, several groins, actually, for you have to be prepared for the 'surgeon' to muck it up and to need a second, third or fourth 'go'.

Dad – Simon Tytherleigh, the Devon-based make-up artist and prosthetics whiz – doesn't always get it right the first time either. Trial and error is the way he and his colleagues have perfected the creation of those amazingly life-like torn, smashed, broken and, of course, bleeding bits of actors' bodies for *Casualty*. Furthermore, it's how they've made them so cheaply.

Let us quickly dispense with a few myths here. It would perhaps be cheaper still if the parts of the bodies caught on camera on the beds, in the cubicles or on the operating tables were actually chunks of meat – a large leg of pork, say, pink and shaved and able to ooze animal blood when the scalpel goes in. It's a technique used on some medical dramas even today. It's not uncommon to find that some TV patients' internal organs are the butcher's best liver and other offal, awful though that sounds to most of us.

On *Casualty* none of this happens. The make-up teams find the idea of using animal flesh distasteful and unhygienic.

Nor, of course, would they ask any of the actors and extras, who are always so keen to appear in *Casualty*, to 'live' the part, be cut, have needles stuck into them or have blood samples syphoned out of them. And if an actor playing a patient hovering between life and death in crash were to have his heart shocked back into action

OPERATION HIT DRAMA

At the warehouse where *Casualty* is made, you often eat lunch next to blokes with 'holes' in their chests or 'bones' sticking out of their legs. Make-up experts like Simon Tytherleigh (below) are offended if you don't stare.

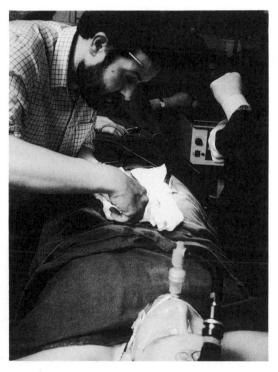

with those defibrilator paddles he'd probably hobble home with a couple of non-faked broken ribs, if he survived at all.

On the contrary, the producers go to great lengths to keep the cast comfortable and ensure that being fatally wounded doesn't hurt a bit. Consequently any syringe seen to press into flesh has been rigged so the needle disappears inside the plunger. When something drastic, an amputation, say, has to be performed, the actor lies on a special board that has a strategically placed hole through which he puts his healthy limb. For the 1992 crossbow injury story the actor whose chest was apparently being opened on the operating table was in fact lying on a false subbed. Yet it was as neat as a Paul Daniels illusion.

Best of all, much of the gunge smeared onto actors is not only non-staining and pleasant-smelling, it's also edible. So the victim of a bomb blast, for example, is painted with blood made mostly from red jelly and tasty maple syrup. If there's brick or cement dust clogging her wounds, uncooked chocolate cake mix is stirred and applied. If she's feeling queasy, poor thing, what she throws up isn't the least bit sour or smelly and won't turn her stomach. It's a concoction of Weetabix, porridge, instant coffee granules, soup or a perfectly palatable dish of the day.

The budget for materials for prosthetics – they include all the ingredients for fake blood, skin, flesh, bones, organs and the generous helpings of vomit we often see, or at least hear – is only a few hundred pounds for most episodes. The falsies have to be specially quick to apply too because *Casualty* does not have the bank balance of a big screen movie which pays for teams of make-up assistants to fuss over each actor. So their illusions have to be pre-planned and prepared so they may be conjured up in moments and require little or no touching up later in the day.

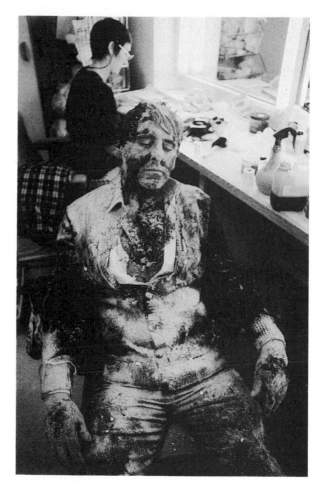

Has this man been buried in rubble?
No, he's been covered in cake-mix

'If you're making *The Elephant Man*, you can stick the actor in a chair and work on him for six or seven hours. Everyone is being paid and there's no panic,' Simon explains.

'In *Casualty* you have two and a half hours at the most, usually nothing like that long, and we know that the artist is far happier if we can keep the process short.'

Strangely, some of the bigger pieces, such as the whole torso or the cyclist's false pelvis, end up taking as little as ten minutes to fix in place.

Tiny cuts and burns can take far, far longer. A whole body, such as the baby needed for the ram-raiding accident episode in the last series, took Simon a week to sculpt in clay. From this he then made silicone and glass fibre moulds. Finally he produced a touchingly life-like little body from solid tinted gelatine.

A few months later he repeated the process for the male baby brought in after drowning in the bath. This time a small latex bladder was buried inside the jelly body. To it was attached a bulb on a long unseen wire. When the infant was resuscitated the doctors, nurses and viewers alike were delighted to see the tiny chest move as breathing started. Simon, crouching out of shot but able to see a monitor, knew when to start squeezing that pump.

It would have been simpler, yes, if the young actress in the ram-raiding story, seen earlier happily sitting in her high chair, had agreed to lie on the table, stay still, be given heart massage and finally act dead. But despite the fears of a few viewers who flinch when children seem to be momentarily unhappy on screen, no Casualty director risks upsetting a tot.

Simon's fifteen-month-old daughter could have saved him hours of work had she agreed to let him take a mould from her, come to that. But she wouldn't keep still long enough, naturally.

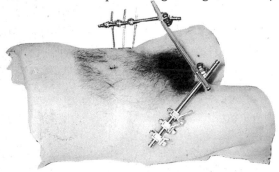

No need to blush. This injured 'cyclist' was a bag of gelatine a week earlier

Better Blood And Gorier Guts

Simon Tytherleigh's colleague Jan Nethercot first cooked up her now famous blood made from jelly when she worked on Threads, the 1984 BBC drama about nuclear war, for which 400 extras had to be made to look gruesomely wounded.

'Obviously I needed gallons of the stuff and the old-fashioned theatrical blood they call Kensington Gore is expensive, stains clothes and it's runny. I just didn't have time to rush round freshening up 400 people,' she says.

'I found if I used gelatine, warm water, a little glycerine with food colouring (basically red with a little green), I could make the blood dribble and it stayed like that all day.'

Jan's recipe is now copied by drama make-up specialists, both professional and amateur. She was asked for the recipe on Jim'll Fix It and when the This Morning programme offered it on Hallowe'en in 1992, the telephone lines were jammed for hours.

But on Casualty they're perfectionists. The blood is dark red if it comes from a vein, bright red if it comes from an artery.

The team didn't invent the use of gelatine for false body bits. It's thought that American make-up artist Dick Smith first developed that idea. Simon, Jan and their colleagues have experimented and improved the mix, adding sorbitol, glycerine, a little zinc and different colourings over the past four years.

'We needed to find something new because most foam latex prosthetics cost a fortune and they also take hours to put on to the actor,' says Simon.

'Gelatine pieces don't crack – which means you can make them and use them weeks later –

Sister Duffy (Catherine Shipton) and gang enjoy their work on an accident victim

and there's the beauty that when you add pigments, the gelatine reflects light like skin does. We use a gelatine that's finer than the commercial stuff with a stronger "bloom".

'The best thing is that jelly cuts and wounds "move". We discovered this when we tried out stitching, which you can't do with latex. One episode had a girl with cuts around her cheek and eye and we were delighted to see that our jelly skin stretched with the suturing and sprang back in just the right way. It meant the director wasn't restricted to one or two movements so it gave him more freedom when he was editing. It also gave the scene a really good dramatic effect.'

The 'laboratory' for these experiments is an unprepossessing unit in the Bristol warehouse, nicknamed 'The Offal Room'. It houses a stack of medical text books with graphic illustrations

Make-up artist Wendy Holmes is one of the inventors in what's nicknamed the 'offal room'

of nightmarish wounds, powdered gelatine in huge sacks, boxes of severed arms, legs, a dead baby or two, and other distressing-looking objects. The equipment is far from sophisticated: fish kettles, pots, pans, spoons, a microwave and an oven.

Planning the wounds and body bits is essential. So Jan, colleagues Sue Kneebone, Wendy Holmes, Derek Lloyd, Chrissie Powers and Simon are among the first people to study the new scripts.

'As soon as we see what the writer has in mind we start looking in our nasty books or ask Peter Salt, our nursing advisor,' says Jan.

The injuries are sometimes first researched by the writers. For the victims of the explosion in the first episode of the 1989 series, the wounds were similar to those observed after the Clapham train crash. Where burns are concerned, one of the make-up team often likes to call in at a couple of burns units to check on the exact shape and colour that a burn from, say, hot fat looks like.

Once designed, the burn is then built up in layers of flesh-tinted gelatine, each one dried with a hair-drier before the next is applied. Swellings, cuts and boils are made in the same way.

'Often the experts disagree about the way wounds should look,' says Jan. 'For the injury to the boy who climbed up the electricity pylon to reach a bird's nest and was electrocuted we were told by one expert that there would be no marks and by other experts that his clothes would have melted into his skin and he'd be badly charred. We thought that sounded more likely and made up the stunt man Nick Powell accordingly.

'We like to get hold of the actors and actresses as soon as we can to make plaster of Paris casts of their faces, or chests, or wherever. Then when we've made the piece we know we can

HOW A HORRIFIC ACCIDENT HAPPENS FOR TELEVISION

Medical student Frances was enjoying an energetic game of squash. Then, in a hellish split second she hit the ball so hard her raquet snapped and she fell, impaling herself in the neck on the spiky handle.

That's what we saw in 'One Step Forward' in series seven. But it took more than a split second for the make-up team and *Casualty*'s real doctor, Dr David Williams, to stage.

First the team made a false torso for actress Suzette Llewellyn. Then make-up assistant Wendy Holmes began to stick a raquet handle on her neck and build up a convincing patch of blood.

Finally, for the cameras, Dr Williams acted removing the stump and tying off the bleeding blood vessels.

It looked as though Julian Chapman was skilfully at work. In fact, Nigel Le Vaillant was more than pleased to stand back, and not have to study Suzette's wounds too deeply. He might easily have fainted and ended up on the next bed.

David says cheerily, 'We had planned to jab the raquet handle into the girl's groin. But we thought it would have been too distressing for the actress and dodgy for the cameras.'

Did the patient survive? 'The man this really happened to did, so Suzette's chances were always good,' he says, with a smile.

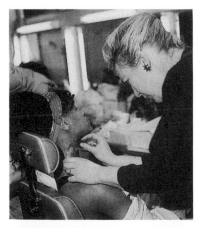

stick it on just before it's needed with the strongest glue.

'If an actor has a very hairy body it can be too much to pull off afterwards. Sometimes we shave them beforehand. Other times we have to sit them in a bath of hot water up to their necks to soak it off.'

One of the team's favourite 'pieces' was the chest they built for wrestler-turned-actor Pat Roach who played a badly injured lorry driver in 1989. Because Pat's a big lad, a chest made of gelatine would have been unbearably heavy. So Simon gathered together all the odds and ends of latex foam he could find ready to stick them into the mould he'd made from the plaster cast.

'It took three of us to lift that plaster cast into the oven and I needed a car jack to open it,' recalls Simon. Pat's own chest was waxed smooth to make removing the fake one less painful. But there was still an awkward side-effect. The glycerine made the poor man's nipples swell and his fellow actors and crew teased him mercilessly.

For especially messy injuries, such as the badly crushed climber's leg with the bone exposed in the first episode of the 1991 series, Simon added beef bones to the gelatine mix for the boy's calf, foot and ankle then, a copy of

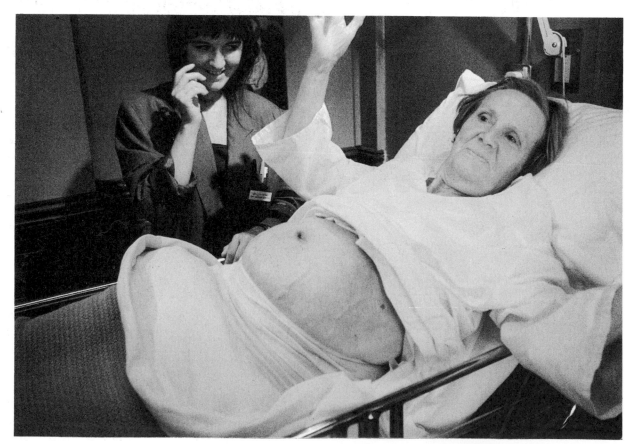

Actress Jean Heywood has a neat, flat tum under the giant mushroom that just landed there

Gray's Anatomy in hand, cut and sculpted a piece of wood for the bone and inserted it into the jelly model, finishing it off with blobs of torn jelly flesh. It was this that actor Nigel Le Vaillant, as Dr Chapman halfway up a mountain, had to steel himself to saw through to amputate the foot.

The team was delighted when Sue Kneebone collected a BAFTA Craft Award for her work on episodes in the 1991 series and has a collective pride in the effects, even if they make squeamish viewers dive behind their settees. Simon admits he was pleased with the girl burned in a boat fire in the 1989 series. They'd kitted out actress Tracy Kneale with a bald cap and a half-bald wig, fake skin to hide a 'lost' eye and a great deal of jelly gore. The result was horrific – enough to make any sailor rush to check the fire precautions on board.

But it's the small details they're most proud of. The way a correctly positioned 'blood vessel' is prepared to spurt at just the right rate as the knife goes in; the small pumping mechanisms that make the murky depths of a body cavity come 'alive' and the way an actor's skin blisters before our very eyes when it accidentally meets acid.

Simon's acid is plain water. But he was pleased with the way it 'burned' in one episode when an actor touched it, raised the hand on which, by then, he'd sprinkled Eno's Fruit Salts mixed with pink colouring which, when sprayed with more water, effervesced into probably the least painful blisters in medical history.

Nevertheless, pain is often felt by viewers at home. Monitoring how much is 'safe' and how much would be too distressing, given that the show is screened at a time on Saturdays when children are likely to be watching, has always been difficult for the producers.

The climber's leg amputation, for example,

was originally filmed to last several seconds but the then Controller of BBC1, Jonathan Powell, ordered that that be curtailed.

'It wasn't just the sight, it was the sound of sawing that turned my stomach and I thought it would affect others the same way,' he said.

That was heartbreaking news for Simon, although he can joke about it now. 'It's not that we like gratuitous gore. It's the technical challenge that drives us. I thought the leg looked terrific, so real. I suppose I liked the idea of long, lingering shots of my work!'

There was some compensation. Simon's leg has become a star turn when members of the make-up team mount exhibitions at shows around Britain. It's introduced as part of the *Casualty* cast.

Geraint Morris reckons he has lopped miles of blood-stained footage from episodes to avoid offending us in his five years with the show. He's strict about sick, too.

'I know that real life nurses who have to pump out patients' stomachs often join in the vomit process themselves. We don't want the same chain reaction to happen to viewers.'

Perhaps it helps to remember that when there is vomit, it's a wholesome variety like the ones 'cooked' up by Jan Nethercot. She reads scripts carefully. 'If it's in an actor it's mine, if not it's props',' she says, laughing.

'We have to know the illness, if there's supposed to be blood in it. That affects the colour. But my basic recipe is chicken broth and Weetabix. Porridge is a good standby. I don't like vegetable soup – the carrots are diced too neatly.'

Jan had one dicey problem with an actress who was due to be sick in a scene. 'She told me she was vegetarian at the last minute. So no chicken broth. I had to rush out to Tesco's for a vegetarian soup.'

The Real Charlie Fairhead—Peter Salt

'People wouldn't dream of walking into a ward where their mum had just had her appendix out and scratching "F.... off" on the wall. Here they don't think twice about it.'

Clinical Nursing Manager Peter Salt is finishing a seven a.m. to three p.m. shift in the accident and emergency department of the Bristol Royal Infirmary. It's a Sunday, so he is not bolting down a late lunch before rushing off to the BBC's warehouse to check that the actors make no mistakes. He has time to talk about what makes his work different from other nursing work.

'The graffiti left on cubicle walls is much like that on the walls of public toilets. People come here and don't pause to think before screaming abuse at nurses just as they're leading someone out whose relatives have been killed. Or chucking chairs around even though there might be someone who's acutely ill in the cubicle.

'They really don't think of this place as a hospital but as an extension of the street. People are often here, still inflamed, often meeting other people they've just been involved with. At night I'd say about 80 per cent of accident cases are drink-related. Drugs are nothing in comparison.'

Sounds like the most unpleasant work place imaginable. Yet there's never a shortage of staff. 'It's probably the only place in a hospital where you genuinely don't know what's happening next. And that's stimulating,' he says.

'Of course there are a lot more sprained ankles and cut fingers than multiple injuries – unlike *Casualty* – but when the big things or the complicated small things do come in, it's

> **They really don't think of this place as a hospital but as an extension of the street.**

actually doing the job you are trained to do which is so satisfying.'

Peter, in his mid-thirties, has perhaps had more reason than others constantly to evaluate his work. For he is the *eminence grise* behind *Casualty*, the man whose opinion is sought first when a new series is being created. Not only does he suggest and advise in the planning and writing stages, he also helps the actors, the make-up and prosthetics designers and attends the filming of the medical scenes at the warehouse to check there are no slip-ups. He also appeared on every programme, although somewhat fuzzily. That was Peter in the white coat, guiding the paramedics rushing a stretcher into Holby in *Casualty*'s opening titles until they were changed for series eight.

Educated in Cornwall, he grew up in Malaysia where his father was serving with the RAF. After taking A Levels and working for a while on a fishing boat, Peter decided to train in psychiatric nursing then moved to Bristol to do his general nursing training. After working in several different departments he started in the accident and emergency ward of the BRI in 1982 and moved through the ranks, becoming in 1992 the department's Clinical Nursing Manager.

It's absolutely no coincidence that after Jeremy Brock and Paul Unwin met Peter in the mid 1980s and *Casualty* was born, Charlie Fairhead's career followed exactly the same pattern as Peter's. As Peter was promoted, Charlie was promoted. When Peter represented colleagues in his union, Charlie did the same. As Peter remained unmarried, dedicated to work, ditto Charlie. But Charlie's affairs, Peter laughs, have been entirely his own. And while Charlie has been duffed up and shot at in the line of duty, Peter has merely been thumped, with no bullet holes yet.

Today the neat, balding professional, who likes to paint and go to the theatre, describes his role in hospital as largely one of troubleshooter. 'You have to develop a knack on a normal day of retaining fifteen things in your head at the same time. You have to know where everyone in the team is and what their problems are.

'But it's often you who is called to do the unpleasant tasks – throwing someone out of the door or dealing with bereaved relatives. I think we'd all say that's the worst of all. You never get used to it.'

When Peter began reading *Casualty* scripts one

Peter Salt: 'Nurses develop a knack of keeping a straight face'

of the things he had to correct most frequently was the way Holby staff gave bad news to patients' relatives. 'These are often the strongest scenes, so I tell writers what I tell junior nurses. You have to say the words "dead" or "died" – there's no point in using euphemisms. On many occasions I've cringed to hear junior doctors saying "The heart stopped" or "He's passed away" because you just know the next question from the relatives will be "But is he going to be all right?" You have to save them from this because the relatives have become the most important people in the department. A few moments earlier their loved one was the highest priority of all. Then the body becomes the lowest priority. By definition it's always sudden death and the relatives won't have had a chance to get used to the idea, so it's always a tense situation.'

Peter admits that despite his years of training he has often felt 'utterly drained' dealing with grief-stricken parents, husbands and wives. 'You sometimes see people leaving alone after being part of a couple for fifty years and they are completely lost. It always affects me.' He points out to all new actors arriving to play nurses and doctors that to dwell on such feelings is a luxury.

'In another few moments you are back sewing up someone's finger or dealing with someone's sore throat – that they've had for three weeks – or, most annoying of all, calming someone who's shouting "Why the bloody hell have I been waiting for three hours?"'

Other mistakes in early scripts that Peter had to correct concerned the relationship between nurses and doctors. 'There is this misconception that nurses are there simply to assist doctors.

Nurses develop a knack of keeping a straight face in the cubicle and exploding two minutes later.

The truth is we work in tandem. I had to keep stressing that our work isn't all about mopping doctors' brows or falling in love with them. Nurses make the majority of the initial clinical decisions. An A & E charge nurse would have had about six years' experience. An A & E doctor, however good or bad, would have had about six months'.

'In those early scripts doctors would be telling nurses what to do all the time, from taking a temperature to taking the patient's clothes off. It's often the other way round, with nurses guiding doctors in the appropriate way. They certainly don't hang around waiting for instruction. A senior nurse in that department is a much bigger fish in a smaller pond than a junior doctor.' Teamwork is perhaps more important in A & E than in any other ward, he believes. 'If you don't work as a team the patients will die.'

The way Peter's work changed when the BRI became a Trust hospital was an important element in shaping the 1992 series in which Holby also became a Trust. Unlike Charlie Fairhead, Peter did not crack up under the pressures but he had to learn to be an accountant, one who controls a £100,000 budget, and to adopt a tough new approach.

'It's not the clinical side against the management exactly – that can work smoothly. It's a matter of Charlie's identifying the things he needs for the department. He mustn't then say, "This is what I'd like ..." but "These are the things I must have for the following reasons." He has to go for it.'

Since that first visit of Brock, Unwin and Geraint Morris, Peter Salt has become an old television hand. He says he's constantly surprised at how unglamorous and slow the work is. 'Standing in a field all night to do one three-minute scene is just grim! And sometimes they spend hours making something and it doesn't appear.' He also feels that the writers dread his responses to their work.

'Both David Williams, a long-time medical consultant to *Casualty*, and I have on occasions had to write back and say "Half of this is garbage". But if 16 million people are watching we have to get it right.'

Peter is pleased he can often include useful hints for viewers who may need to do first aid in an emergency. He has often suggested scenes which demonstrate how to help an accident victim lie down protecting the neck, how to stop bleeding by direct pressure (no tourniquets, please) and to treat burns with water or ironed clothing which is usually sterile. He's also keen that the show emphasises the dangers of over-the-counter drugs such as paracetamol.

There are some aspects of real A & E life that Peter would not want to see reflected in *Casualty*, though. 'There can be some hilarious things. Not just patients coming in with bottles stuck up their backsides. But a tremendous amount of black humour, a lot of background mickey-taking, about funny hairstyles, crazy clothes, voices and the stories people have to tell. Nurses develop a knack of keeping a straight face in the cubicle and exploding two minutes later. But if the writers tried to include it, it would look insensitive because the cases are often tragic too.'

What would make Peter Salt give up nursing? 'I certainly won't be going into television full time,' he says. 'But when I deal with someone who has fallen off a skyscraper and then go off to eat my dinner without thinking twice about it, when I feel it isn't touching me at all, I'll know it's time to quit.'

The First Real Casualty Doctor— David Williams

A cut took Dr David Williams to *Casualty* – a hair cut. The cutter was an old friend from David's school who had been trimming script editor Caroline Oulton's hair. Chatting, as you do, she mentioned that she needed a 'tame' medic to advise and monitor the operations and procedures for the drama series she was working on. The hairdresser mentioned it to David.

'She came to watch me work at Whipps Cross Hospital in East London where I was a Casualty Officer and gave me Jeremy Brock and Paul Unwin's first scripts,' says the thirty-one-year-old publican's son who'd qualified only a year earlier at the London Hospital in Whitechapel. A visit to BBC Television Centre in White City, where the first Holby was carefully built and dismantled every few weeks, left Dr David 'wide-eyed' and intrigued. So began the physician's other, secret life: his treatment of the healthy to make them appear to be at death's door.

'I read the scripts and thought, hmm, some basic mistakes here, I could make it more accurate and even more exciting. I knew nothing about television. I think I'd once caught an episode of *Angels* and I hadn't taken it seriously. But I didn't think the *Casualty* stories were shocking or too outrageous because I'd already discovered that anything can happen. I'd been working in the casualty department in Whitechapel during the Wapping riots. The injured policemen were brought in to us (the injured pickets went to Bart's). Anyway, you don't have to be there long to encounter the drunks and all the aggressive, awful, ungrateful people who turn up.

'I didn't think those first scripts were especially political, either. They were trying to portray reality and in hospitals the staff, like any other employees, will complain about their employers. That's how things were. Doctors and nurses are bright people, they can see ways of improving things. I've often spent half a shift on the phone trying to find a bed for a patient. And I've also rung an administrator at three in the morning to complain.

'As for the way it portrayed doctors – Baz taking amphetamines to keep her going – well, I realized this wasn't a programme that was adoring of doctors. They weren't the great heroes. But no doctor can honestly come to me and say this doesn't happen.

'But what the writers got wrong then, and sometimes now, is the timing. They want to portray someone who's nearly dead, then getting better, then walking out of the door, all in the same hospital shift. You really can't press illness into that time scale.'

David Williams' career until then, he believes, was fairly typical of most docs who, like Baz, Beth or Rob, decide to see what it's like on the front line. 'Casualty is often a doctor's first job after registration when he or she hasn't made a decision about the future. It's a good place to help you make up your mind because there's a bit of everything,' David says. Because of these doctors' inexperience and sometimes their naiveté, it's often the nurses who seem to be running the place. 'I can remember going to them and asking what to do next. They can be quite the hardest and most cynical bunch of people, casualty nurses. They have to be, dealing with so many ungrateful shits on Friday or Saturday nights. They'd crack up otherwise.'

David's aim was to make the medical problems and the solutions to them intriguing and different. He found, too, that he often had to do bits of the acting, or rather his gloved hands did, because actors, however hard they practised, simply couldn't make it look as though they used those instruments every day of their lives.

'I included procedures never shown on TV before,' he says with pride. 'One was a chest drain – for someone who has air around the lung. I also showed them how to put a wire into the heart to draw off blood and how to do cardiac pacing. Then there were simple things like putting patients on ventilators and defibrilating, giving them shocks, a bit of an old favourite now.' He also learned which illnesses writers liked – because of their dramatic possibilities. 'They love the extradural haematoma – we've done it several times now – when a patient is knocked out, then there's a lucid interval and then they go unconscious again suddenly and either die or are saved by quick action. In the lucid period, of course, they will have told their loved ones something amazing.'

David soon began to help with the structuring of the medical scenes and he also wrote the medical dialogue. 'Writers tried to get away with "Pass the scalpel, nurse" or "He's out of danger". Doctors don't say that. We talk in a matter-of-fact way, normally, we don't use that many medical terms. I was taking the melodrama out of the scripts. The writers were sometimes upset and I was upset, well, irritated, when my notes were ignored and it was all grossly inaccurate. Writing for this series is hard, you have to conform and keep within the confines of the running story. Many otherwise good writers just can't cope.'

Over his seven years with Casualty, David has

> # I realized this wasn't a programme that was adoring of doctors.

suggested dozens of storylines. Some have proved to be a headache to film. One was the idea, based on a true case, of a boy who'd been having a tooth filled at the dentist's and inhaled the drill head. David suggested that the boy had asthma so the need for surgery was urgent. 'In casualty they could see it on the X-ray. What was needed was a bronchoscopy, a tube put into the lung to grab things out. The director was worrying about the apparent sight of a patient having to swallow a horrible tube. The dentist was panicking because he hadn't put a guard at the back of the mouth. It was all very difficult.' One difficult operation turned out on screen to

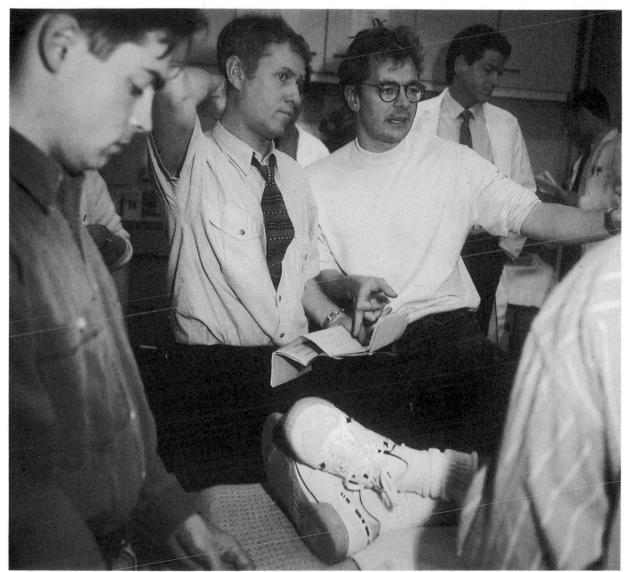

Dr David Williams (in specs) shows actor Derek Thompson and the crew how it might happen for real

look admirably authentic, David recalls. It was a spleen removal on a small girl following the bomb explosion in 'Hanging On'. 'We spent hours getting this right with Julian Glover, who played the surgeon. It was brilliant. But it was never seen. Peter Cregeen, then the Head of Drama Series, thought it too painful to watch!'

Some scenes that were screened gave David pain, notably an early episode which showed a young woman who was brain dead after a car crash. She carried a donor card and was being whipped off to have her organs removed just as her parents arrived. They saw that she was still being ventilated and thought she was going for a life-saving operation. They didn't know she was dead. 'Well, it was all just possible, sort of. I had been too soft allowing them to compress the time,' says David. 'As a result the UK Transplant Service people were immediately in touch with the BBC, enraged at the way it seemed to them that we were showing victims being rushed off to remove organs. I wrote back justifying it but I felt uneasy. Then to my delight, three months later the transplant people wrote back to say "You'll be pleased to know there has not been a fall off in organ donors." The whole thing made me sit up straight and realize how responsible my job was. I realized that this isn't playing.'

David later suggested another organ donor story in 'Living Memories' which he believes had a positive message. It was that of a young boy who was knocked off his bicycle and suffered head injuries which left him brain dead. His father refused permission for him to become an organ donor. On the following day he returned to say he'd changed his mind. By then,

Writers tried to get away with "Pass the scalpel, nurse" or "He's out of danger". Doctors don't say that.

tragically, it was too late. 'We have to be very careful in dealing with such matters as organ transplant, Aids, child abuse and other social issues. I think it's important to educate as well as entertain. That's why in series four when there'd been publicity about people with Aids looking perfectly normal, I was keen to show it's a fatal disease with a nasty, painful death.

'We've tried to show doctors being negligent too,' says David. 'Rob, for instance, starts by throwing his weight around, makes mistakes and has to be corrected.'

David was concerned in the early days that *Casualty* was nurse-heavy. 'There never seemed to be enough doctors. Ewart Plimmer was very much a hands-off consultant. I suggested they have a Registrar who has three or four years more experience than a houseman. So that's how Julian came on the scene.'

Julian's departure prompted a 'long confrontation' between David and the script editors. David thought it made no sense for him to quit in a huff. 'He had just been made a consultant and doctors usually strive for about twelve years to reach this pinnacle, a job that is usually for life. Yet in the course of a couple of episodes we found that he was so exasperated, he resigned. Julian was bad at fighting and all consultants have to fight their corner. Few consultants can afford to quit, anyway, unless they have independent means.' Finally a compromise was reached and viewers learned that Julian had by a lucky chance found another job.

David Williams also quit *Casualty* last autumn. He had recently married and was engrossed in his 'day' job, as a nephrologist at London's

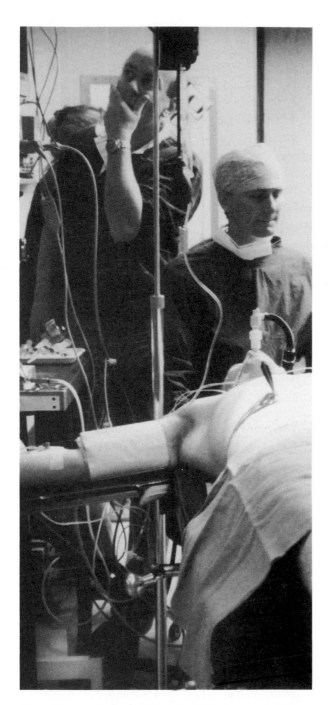

Casualty's **new medical advisor, Geoff Hughes, doesn't like the look of that shot on the monitor**

University College Hospital researching into medical disorders during pregnancy. He'd also found himself advising on many other television programmes, including *Trainer*, *EastEnders*, *A Very Peculiar Practice* and *Medics*. Geoff Hughes, the A & E Consultant at the Bristol Royal Infirmary, who didn't have to spend hours on the motorway to get to Holby, has taken over David's work.

David says he has been mocked mercilessly by colleagues who knew of his 'moonlighting' at Holby. 'I used to get it in the neck on Monday mornings after the show went out if there'd been an X-ray put up the wrong way, or if it showed the wrong bit of the body. These things usually happened when I wasn't on set. Doctor friends would also point out that the actors pressed too gingerly on someone's chest or seemed to take too long to do something!' On the other hand, he confesses to 'bristling with pride' when a patient revealed she'd learned about her illness from watching the show. 'She was thought to have meningitis and it was necessary for her to have a lumbar puncture. I began to explain it to her and she said "You don't have to tell me, I've just seen it on *Casualty*".' He also had a patient who diagnosed his own thombosis in the leg after watching an episode. Before it, he'd thought he had merely strained a muscle.

David hopes to write for *Casualty* in future and laughs at the prospect of Geoff sending him brusque notes about medical accuracy. 'It will be galling,' he says.

After seven years of involvement with a fictional hospital department, he is still down-to-earth. 'The truth is, you patch them up and throw them out. The programme credits the *Casualty* staff with sorting out the medical and social problems of so many patients. In reality that can't happen.'

Clive Haddrell—The Real Paramedic

'It looks so easy to lift a trolley in and out of an ambulance, doesn't it?' says Clive Haddrell. 'But actors never have a clue. There was one occasion when a couple of them playing the paramedics were lifting a famous actress taking a guest role and they did it so badly, she fell off.'

Clive, of the new Paramedic Motorcycle Response Unit of the Avon Ambulance Trust, was called in to save more of Casualty's stars from developing real bruises and to make the dramas at the scenes of accidents absolutely accurate.

'In the early days I don't think the BBC appreciated the skills of paramedics. They thought the only thing we did was drive the ambulances and that only the doctors and nurses were important to the patients. So in the first episodes there were lots of mistakes. Yet it's so important to show viewers what's technically correct – you wouldn't want someone to get the wrong idea, it could cost a life.'

Thanks to his input, millions will have learned, for instance, that it's dangerous to remove a road accident victim's crash helmet if he or she is lying injured and may have a damaged neck or spine. They've learned what's most important in those first moments: talking to the patient; getting as full a picture as possible of his or her condition; calming the relatives; and acting fast if the heart has stopped, blood is being lost or the pain is severe. Being a whiz at the wheel when lights are flashing and the siren blaring comes a long way down the list.

West Country man Clive, who's in his forties, qualified as an electrician at a nuclear power station after leaving school. Perhaps because he was an ambulance man's son he took over the responsibility for first aid at work and slowly his interest in that grew. 'I also realized that the type of job where you'd never know from one day to the next what you'd be up against and who you'd be meeting was exciting – that's why I switched and joined the ambulance service.'

Since Casualty was first screened, many more young men and women have been drawn to the work. They're not put off by the rigorous training, which includes studying for anatomy and physiology exams, observation and practical work in hospitals, learning how to administer drugs, developing communication skills as well as taking the Road Craft courses which the police also use.

Doctors used to treat ambulance staff as menials.

'If you get through all that, you have to re-qualify every three years,' Clive continues with a chuckle. 'So it's a lot more than fast driving.'

He'd certainly consider Ian Bleasdale and Caroline Webster, who play Holby paramedics Josh and Jane, as recruits. 'They've both got the right attitudes, they work together and they're flexible. Ian keeps copying me with the "All right, my love?" remarks to people playing patients. It gives my colleagues a laugh.'

Since 1986 Clive has trained a steady stream of actors to act and sound like him and, like Peter Salt, he too featured in the old titles – he was the hazy figure in the back of the ambulance. 'They find it helpful to come out with a team for a day. Some find some of the sights too painful but they usually cope.'

He is also on call to advise writers and he casts a stern eye over the filming of accident scenes and the stunts for several days of each

Clive Haddrell (centre), the paramedic advisor who's Josh's role model

episode's production. He believes *Casualty* has reflected the changes in paramedics' skills and their role in health care.

'Doctors used to treat ambulance staff as menials. Ewart Plimmer, in the early episodes, used to look down on Mute and Ponting and that was realistic then. Doctors were gods. But over the years they've realized that it makes sense to take the treatment to the patient and we've improved our skills accordingly. In fact I have been asked to lecture groups of doctors on what *they* can do at the scene of an accident. What I tell them amounts to this — offer to help but if you come over all dictatorial, there'll be trouble!'

In twenty years Clive has seen almost every variation of murder, suicide, electrocution, hanging, overdosing, burning, mishap and mangling in motor vehicles. 'I've been in the thick of some dreadful riots. I've seen youths on the rampage like they showed in the last episode of the last series of *Casualty*. I've been physically attacked — even though you're wearing an ambulance jacket, you still become a victim — and yes, I do get depressed by it. It's not necessarily the gory sights.

'It's sometimes the way people treat each other, poor people and rich people, who can be a pain in the rear with their complaints that you aren't doing enough. There are things I couldn't tell anyone about, not even my wife. But the stress is short-lived. Some ambulance people keep this close to them and that can be foolish. Luckily a stress counsellor is just starting to be available to us.

'But the worst headache I have is from these television types — they don't give me a moment's peace,' he adds, deadpan. Then roars with laughter.

Luckily Clive now shares his advisory work with other colleagues in the Avon Ambulance Trust.

Unit B6—The Real Holby

You wouldn't dream of taking your sick child or your football team's bleeding centre forward to the real A & E department of Holby Hospital. The best they could do for you there is find you an Elastoplast.

What we see on screen as Holby's entrance, gardens and exterior is actually part of Bristol's Brunel Technical College. Sometimes the dramatic operations we watch are performed in real operating theatres of the Bristol Royal Infirmary on days when they're not needed by real patients.

But the rest, which looks so like local NHS hospitals up and down the land, is actually part of a grey and unexceptional warehouse on an industrial estate in Bristol. There are no peaked-capped BBC doormen, no frills of any kind. Outside, among the cars and vans, you might spot a small catering truck in which two or three people conjure up hot meals for a multitude. Inside, sitting at long rows of tables or chatting by the tea urns and plastic cups are the busy crew and those cast members called that day. Some of them, playing patients, may be tucking hungrily into their grub despite apparently gushing wounds or deathly pallor. Portakabins on two levels make adequate 'green' rooms and rest rooms, offices for the production staff and workrooms for the make-up and costume departments. Usually there's a hum of conversation, the sound of a TV set tuned to the day's sport and the occasional buzz of a bell signifying that cameras are rolling.

Where they're rolling is beyond a heavy blue door, in a different world. Here are the examination cubicles. There are four real ones and three or four more which are merely the curtains (green until series seven, then grey) and conceal blank walls or piles of cable and other filming equipment. Backing this area is the familiar wide reception counter made in best plywood behind which Norma Sullivan asks the dying for their postcodes. On the desk tops, computer screens flicker and a very small number of record cards are scattered around. In front is the hall where the patients and their relatives wait on rows of plastic chairs. At one side is a box of toys, a pile of old magazines. To the right of the entrance doors is a 'refreshment' area, a couple of tables and chairs near a hot drinks machine, a fully stocked snack machine and a row of telephone boxes. It's through here that patients on trolleys are rushed to the crash room and to the alcove where staff write up notes, take phone calls, shuffle folders of notes and look at X-rays.

Back outside near the telephones are the stairs leading to the balcony, Charlie's office, the staff room with its lockers and battered armchairs, Mike Barratt's office and signs pointing to an X-Ray department which doesn't exist.

Everything, down to the dull cream and blue paint, looks authentic. The tranquillisers and antibiotics are vitamin pills but the beds, bedding and all the other props here are authentic hospital issue, obtained from medical equipment suppliers or loaned by the manufacturers.

The equipment is kept up-to-date too. In the case of the ECG heart monitor and portable ventilator we see, they're state of the art. In fact, it saddens Peter Salt to think that these sophisticated machines could be working to save lives at his own hospital. 'At the Bristol Royal Infirmary we have much older models. It's hard for me to think of them not being put to good use when the cameras are not on them.'

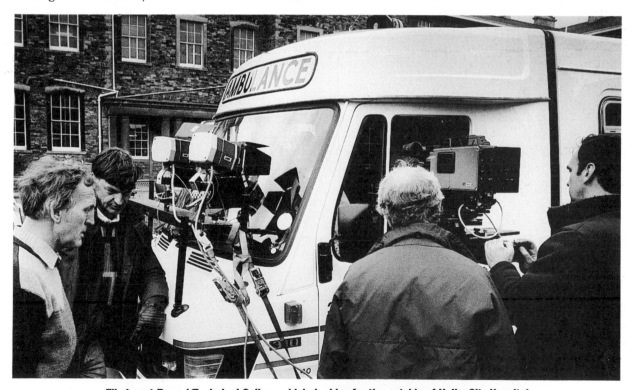

Filming at Brunel Technical College which doubles for the outside of Holby City Hospital

HICCUPS

Even in the best planned operations there can be complications. But even when *Casualty* seems problem-free to producers, eagle-eyed viewers pounce.

All *Casualty* stories are based on true cases. The medical experts offer suggestions. Writers, who include a former police Chief Inspector, former teachers and former actors, draw on their experiences and their research. Sometimes viewers contribute ideas. A young mother, for instance, offered her story of how she was suspected of battering her baby when the baby actually had brittle bones. It became a storyline for writer Ginnie Hole.

Complications can arise in any operation, though, and making entertaining drama means taking the risk of touching sensitive nerves and treading on innocent toes. And they needn't be human toes. *Casualty* committed a howler in November 1991 when it hired a Staffordshire Bull Terrier in a non-barking role as a potentially dangerous dog. The implication of the story was clearly that the hound was a pit bull terrier involved in vicious fights. After the episode was shown the production office was swamped with angry letters from vets, Staffordshire bull terrier societies and from individual owners, many of whom enclosed snaps of docile pets, most of them detailing the differences between the two breeds. Geraint Morris could only apologise for the mistake: the animal agency which supplied the performing canine had assured them that 'no one would know the difference'. When the episode, 'Making the Break', was repeated as many dog shots as possible had been edited out. It's worth adding that the dog in the story, Pit Bull or Staffordshire, was a decoy and entirely innocent. Its master was the dangerous animal.

A year later another doggy problem presented itself for *Casualty*. 'Body and Soul' was to tell a cautionary tale about the accidents that may occur when anti-blood-sports campaigners and

A horse plays dead and some non-registered foxhounds give the crew a run for their money

foxhunters clash in the excitement of the chase. Location Manager Annie Hutchinson recalls: 'We had set things up with the Berkeley Hunt in Gloucestershire to use their dogs. The members there were also helping us with the script. But at the last minute the Hunt Masters' Association heard about it and feared that the story would be biased against hunters. They instructed all their members that they weren't to co-operate in any way. We tried dozens but no one could help. Finally, we were lucky and found a pack of fox-hounds in Wales which was not registered. The Forestry Commission eventually agreed that we could use some land near Chepstow and a local riding school provided horses and young riders.'

Peter Bowker's script had a young hunt sabo-teur killed when a horse jumped a log and hit him on the head. An elderly rider was injured too. The horse would break a leg and have to be shot. 'We had a specially trained horse for the death scene,' says Annie. 'Its trainer pressed its withers, held the reins and gave it a special sign so that it slowly lay down. There was no gun in sight. It got up happily moments later, of course.' In the post on the following Monday morning there were loads of letters from wor-ried viewers concerned about the 'poor' beast.

Animal rights campaigners were already attacking *Casualty* before another episode, 'Act of Faith', was even filmed. The story, about a spec-tacular fall from a trapeze which happens after two young artists foolishly go ahead with their act despite being under-rehearsed, was set in a traditional circus, where elephants and bears, including polar bears, were also to be seen per-forming. Rula Lenska played the whip-lashing owner of her family-owned circus, actually Fosset's Circus, on tour in the summer of 1992 and pitched in Cobham, Surrey. The *Casualty* team had had to publicize their presence to attract an audience inside the circus tent for the

filming day and, predictably, there was an angry protest demonstration. When fists began flying, a photographer from the local paper was knocked down and Rula, an active member of the elephants' welfare group Elefriends, was the object of much shouting and hate-mail. She revealed later that she'd agonized over taking the role, decided that work was work (and she needed it) and that she'd asked not to be filmed in shots with animals.

'*Casualty* is the most compelling series on tele-vision and I've always wanted to be in it, so when the part was offered I had to make a major decision,' she said. She added that the work had modified her views about circus ani-mals. 'I still don't like the idea of wild animals being kept in captivity for the entertainment of humans. But they are not punished, they are looked after with great love and affection. There is also the fact that these animals are second or third generation captive-bred. There is no way they could be put back into the wild.'

Despite the demo, the circus show went on. That wasn't the case when the team travelled to Barmouth in Wales to film 'Making Waves'. This is the episode where Dr Rob (Jason Riddington) goes off to relax on a luxury cruiser clumsily handled by friends played by Martin Jarvis and his wife Rosalind Ayres. The couple mis-read the tides, the cruiser is grounded and then wrecked and the passengers have to sink or swim. The location manager had decided against filming in the nearby Severn Estuary because the waters there can be treacherous. Instead he chose the sea off Barmouth, mid Wales.

As usual a storyboard artist read the script and drew the story scene by scene. (This enables the director, cameraman, soundman, actors, cos-tume, make-up and props people to know exact-ly what's needed when and how each scene, often shot out of sequence, fits into the jigsaw.)

Also as usual, the days of location filming were elaborately planned, schedules made, hotels booked, insurance policies taken out, vehicles and equipment hired. What no one had foreseen was that the owner of the hired smart boat, valued at more than £20,000, would become anxious and object to the potential damage to his craft when he saw how the filming was proceeding. He could not be reassured that while his boat might be seen to shudder, the actual boat that would crash would be a model in a studio. The owner cancelled the arrangement and the forty-strong BBC team consequently had to pack up, return to their Bristol base and, when a second similar cruiser could be found and hired, return and repeat the whole process. Not surprisingly, the episode is not one the team discusses except through clenched teeth.

Glad to be back on dry land – the ship-wrecked stars of 'Making Waves'. And the *Casualty* crew, for different reasons

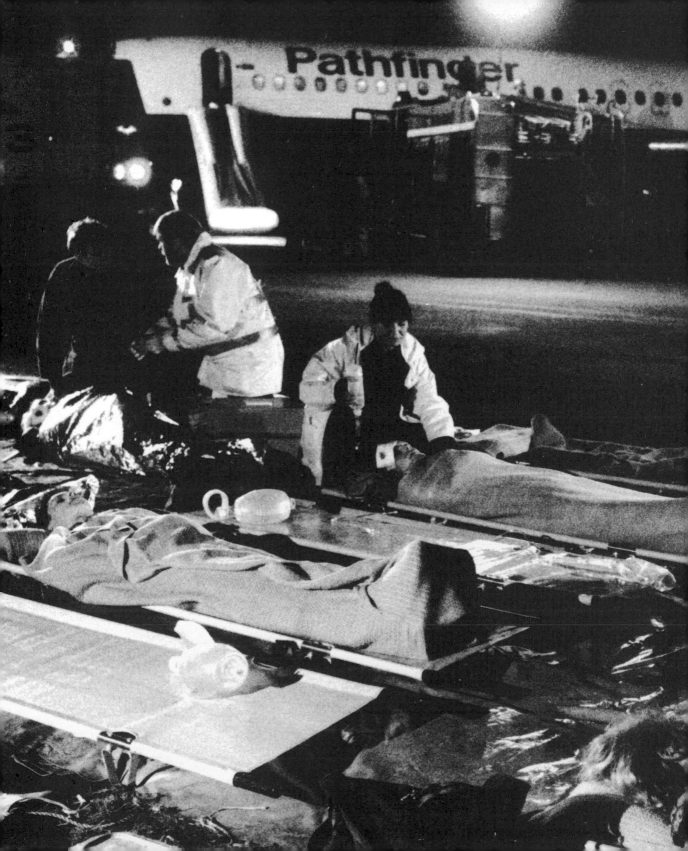

By contrast 'Cascade', the episode in which an aircraft was wrecked near the fictional Holby Airport, is a firm favourite. No one compares the effects produced with those you'd expect in a big-budget Hollywood epic, but for ingenuity in using three different planes as well as models and the flight simulator at Gatwick, it deserves its own craft Oscar.

'We knew we couldn't afford to crash a plane,' says Edwina Craze, associate producer for series six and seven who worked with designer Andrew Purcell on this episode. 'We knew there was a plane grounded at Bristol airport, a Trident. It's old but luckily the type is still flying. The inside had been ripped out because it's used for training by students at Brunel College of Technology. We knew we could shoot the outside of it. We searched everywhere for an interior and finally found one at the museum at RAF Wroughton. We had to update the seats and the logos.

'For the shots when our plane was coming into the airport and everything was going wrong we filmed in a ten-seater as it landed at Bristol Airport. We made a model of a plane hitting trees and a grassy bank with its undercarriage collapsing.'

'Cascade' almost crashed into viewing oblivion, though, when its screening in December 1991 had to be postponed in order not to clash with the anniversary of the Lockerbie crash. The postponement caused complaints from viewers, some of whom felt it should have been shown while others felt the producers should have spotted the unfortunate timing earlier. After it was shown in March 1992 it incurred the wrath of a group of doctors at a Liverpool hospital because it showed the Holby gang going back on duty after drinking alcohol at a party to treat the

The crash in 'Cascade' took four different planes

crash victims. No doctor or nurse should go on duty unless sober, they said.

Luckily *Casualty*'s dramatic licence has not been confiscated but few disgruntled *Casualty* viewers suffer in silence. Receptionists have complained that Holby's Norma was an attack on them. Radiologists have complained the script often has Holby doctors (unfairly) bemoaning the time it takes for X-rays to be sent up to them. Hospital chaplains have complained that Holby doesn't have one and physiotherapists are aching to be represented in some heroic light. Football club

No football league stadium wanted to allow the *Casualty* team to film scuffles

managers blacklisted *Casualty* before they'd read Ginnie Hole's script for 'Penalty' depicting Hillsborough-like chaos at a game. Finally, the riot scenes were shot at a non-league stadium in Newport, Wales, and then only after a number of local football supporters had been placated. Bell-ringers wanted to bring back the rope for Stephen Wyatt, writer of 'Profit and Loss'. They telephoned and wrote in after he had a patient reporting a medley of minor mishaps suffered while ringing some bells. Stephen had learned of the potential injuries (some of which sound comical to non-ringers) from a long list in *The Guardian* but viewers with campanology experience regretted that the episode could have made the already difficult job of recruiting volunteers even harder. Anyway, they said, no one is left dangling 30 feet in the air in well-run belfries.

But it's not all complaints. There are many dramatically positive side-effects of viewing *Casualty* on record, too. Countless people must have absorbed the correct way to revive people who collapse unexpectedly after watching *Casualty* paramedics perform their life-saving tasks. One was vet Anne Lowe. She was able to give the kiss of life and heart massage to a pensioner who had a heart attack while shopping in Paignton, Devon, last year, skills she attributes to regular visits to Holby. Nuclear power worker Donald Sexton diagnosed a potentially deadly thrombosis in a lung and one of his legs after watching a 1987 *Casualty* episode in which a man was taken into hospital complaining of breathlessness, chest and leg pains. Donald, then forty-one, recognised the symptoms as similar to his own, saw his doctor the following week and was subsequently admitted to a hospital in Chester for surgery. His wife wrote to the programme thanking them for saving his life.

In April 1993 a liver transplant operation, performed on a twenty-five-year-old woman

PLOTTING THE CRASHES AND SMASHES

A lorry driver had fallen asleep at the wheel. His vehicle, veering wildly out of control, ploughed through an estate agent's window. A man who was looking in the window was rammed through it.

The man the viewers glimpsed was an actor. The one being hurled through the glass, was Tip Tipping, the late, great stunt man.

The man who choreographed that accident, one of hundreds in the history of Holby A & E, was Gareth Milne, himself a 'victim' in dozens of *Casualty* episodes. He is also the man who for seven series planned and arranged all the disasters that have made us wince and, he hopes, try to avoid for real.

Gareth, like Tip, does not boast about the daredevil aspects of the trade. 'I'm a functionary. I'm very serious and take pride in my safety record,' says the Wales-based former sailor, who has worked on scores of feature films, doubled for Dennis Waterman in *The Sweeney* and arranged stunts on umpteen television series since.

'Stunt work is about being able to judge time and distance and about being honest. Most things that I'm presented with in a script are achievable but some aren't. You have to say, "No, that can't be done". If I did everything a director asked

The unseen stars – stunt drivers causing exciting chaos in 'Chain Reaction'

me to do, I'd be dead and so would a lot of other people.'

It was Gareth's job not only to instruct the stunt team but also to check and recheck the equipment and the buffers, such as the elaborate mountain of cardboard boxes on to which the stunt artist Lucy Allen fell during the scary trapeze scene in 'Act of Faith'.

But how, for example, did the motorcyclist in 'Cry Wolf' hit a car head-on, fly over the bonnet, fall, get dragged along the road, bang his head against the kerb and (when the cameras weren't on him) get up, brush himself down and enjoy a refreshing cup of tea? Gareth was that motorcyclist. 'As usual the car that's supposed to be going at 50 mph is only going at about 12 mph. The camera angles are flatter so it's not obvious. I did the collision and fall in four separate pieces. When I was scraped across the

road, I was actually on a piece of hardboard and a cable was pulling me along.'

Tip Tipping was the main stunt man in the elaborate 'Chain Reaction' tumbling toxic drums episode. But Gareth remembers him most clearly in the runaway lorry crush. 'The window was in three panes, the outer two were glass and the middle one was sugar glass which breaks easily and doesn't cut,' explains Gareth. 'In the shot the man is stationary but in fact Tip was running backward for about 50 yards with the lorry behind him. At the last minute, he turned and faced the lorry and jumped backwards into the shop. Then he rolled on the floor pulling a black cloth over him. We had to do it in one take. We only had one lot of sugar glass.'

The stunt co-ordinators for series eight are Stuart St Paul and Dave Holland.

who had only three days to live without it, might not have gone ahead but for the fact that *Casualty* is the favourite television series of Royal Navy diver John Ravenhall. A Cessna aircraft ferrying the donated organ from Birmingham to Edinburgh crashed into reclaimed land and ditched into the waters of the Firth of Forth in the early hours of the morning. Seaman Ravenhall, known as Yo-Yo, swam below the plane's wings, entered the plane and eventually found the picnic-hamper-style box containing the organ wrapped in its ice pack, in the fuselage. He recognized it, having seen similar boxes on *Casualty*. He was able to bring it out safely and in time for the transplant surgery to be performed. 'You see this sort of container on *Casualty* when you see police bringing them to the hospital,' the delighted twenty-four-year-old seaman hero said later.

There has also been a case of *Casualty* shooting itself in the foot. Interviewed on television in March 1992 after Sue Kneebone accepted the BAFTA Craft Award for the show's make-up, proud producer Geraint Morris stood by an X-ray box at the Bristol set explaining that the show's most important consideration was its authenticity. Medically speaking, they did not make mistakes.

Unfortunately, more than one doctor watching noticed that the chest X-ray in the box was either the wrong way round or the patient was one of those rare people whose heart is on the right. Whoops!

Writing for *Casualty*

Ginnie Hole has developed an allergy since writing for *Casualty*. She can't take doctors. 'A lot of the ones I've met are far more patronizing than even Julian Chapman was when he began,' she says. 'Of course some are nice, clever and sensi-tive. But on the whole my vet is far more sympathetic about the state of my dog than any doctor has ever been about the state of me or my family. Looking back, I think *Casualty* has shown doctors and the Health Service in far too favourable a light.'

Ginnie, who has been one of the main writers on the show from 1987 onwards, bases her opinions on five years as a sort of hospital groupie. In that time she regularly left the comfort of her home at supper time to hang around accident and emergency departments all night long. There, notebook in hand, often in a borrowed white coat, she peeked behind cubicle curtains, chatted to doctors, nurses, porters, reception staff, ambulance men, policemen and of course patients. She watched the way they behaved together and those observations have formed the basis of the sixteen episodes she has written.

'When I first started to go, the nurses were furious with me because they thought the early episodes of *Casualty* made them seem wacky and silly. I didn't necessarily agree but I realized that we had to do more research and be as accurate as possible. I asked as many questions as I could. In the early years I was having to pay a babysitter, so I felt I had to work hard to justify it!'

Her resolution to make her stories authentic soon began to show – in her phone bills. Before *Casualty*, Ginnie had written for *Angels*, the twice-weekly drama largely about the lives of student nurses. 'My O level biology got me through. I topped it up with about one or two inquiries on medical matters an episode,' she laughs. 'For *Casualty* I talked endlessly to our medical advisors. It accounted for about £150 of my phone bills each quarter.'

The more she talked to the experts, the more she felt she knew the stories they preferred – and those that put their blood pressure up. 'I'm afraid I've played tricks on David Williams. I've

Writer Ginnie Hole (right), accepts the Royal Television Society's Best Drama award in 1992

say something about the Health Service. But you can only do so much. What's happening in other hospital departments now is actually much more worrying. Casualty departments have to stay open. But others can just be closed, no patients admitted, when the money runs out. I feel I want to stand up and scream about it.' For this reason Ginnie is now developing drama projects which she hopes will reflect the wider picture of the Health Service.

There's already hot competition for Ginnie's place in the team among the country's top scriptwriters. For any aspiring candidates, here's how it all happens:

Holby Hospital comes to life in stages. The first is a planning meeting for the new series attended by the producer, his two script editors, the medical advisors and some of the writers. The talk ranges from new trends in the Health Service and medical techniques to the availability of the show's leading actors, ideas for new characters, outlines of topics which might be covered and, of course, budgets.

The script editors then go away, devise a master plan and compose rough outlines of the stories concerning the Holby staff for each episode. The fate of Charlie, Duffy and their colleagues rests with them. Then individual writers who have asked to write on, say, domestic violence or tensions in a factory, or are known to be passionate about an issue, are pencilled in to create the stories about the patients.

'You try to make the staff stories and the patients' off-set each other,' says Ginnie. 'From your notes you do a scene-by-scene treatment of the episode. I usually end up with cards all over the floor as I move the order around.' Then the writing starts. Most writers spend around two months completing a script. It can be lonely and the re-writing can be frustrating. With or without gangrene.

written in cod scenes of doctors and nurses making mad, passionate love – just to alarm him!'

The work was playing tricks on her, too. 'I was a hypochondriac before. But it got much worse. I think I imagined I was developing almost every disease I wrote about. When I gave a patient gangrene, I had pins and needles in my feet the whole time I was writing!'

The research must have worked because the nurses she met, along with other Health Service workers who watched, began to concede that the series was 'on their side'. From her end, though, Ginnie says she felt her early faith in the NHS ebbing away.

'Four years ago I felt we were really able to

CASENOTES

Is there an accident, an illness, a social problem that hasn't revealed itself yet behind the grey cubicle curtains of Holby City's A & E ward? Here's a way of checking: brief summaries of every episode shown so far with a few reminders of which guest actors were lurking under the blood, sweat and tears.

EPISODE 1 — GAS
by Jeremy Brock and Paul Unwin

At Holby docks, a drum of toxic gas falls on two dockers. One dies, the other suffers a badly burned leg. Other workers are poisoned and the team – Doctors Ewart and Baz, nurses Charlie, Clive, Megan and Duffy – is on standby. Megan warns Clive about his drinking habits, while Ewart has trouble with a regular drunk. A young girl is forced to drink milk after drinking car fluid, and a stubborn man being treated after being hit on the head by a golf ball annoys Charlie. It's porter Kuba and receptionist Susie who manage to identify the illegal toxin, which harmed the dockers, by its smell of garlic.

EPISODE 2 — HIDE AND SEEK
by Jeremy Brock and Paul Unwin

Two young girls playing on a railway line are picked up by ambulance team Andrew Ponting and Sandra Mute when one suffers a head injury after falling from a bridge. Megan criticizes Baz for allowing a pregnant mother, who wants her birth induced for convenience, to be admitted. A strange woman turns up in reception with a baby (which she had snatched from its real mother earlier) in her arms. She locks herself in the toilets and threatens to stab the infant with a pair of scissors. Baz handles the situation calmly, but the baby is already dead. A DHSS inspector comes in to see the staff in action and is unimpressed. A man who thinks he has had a heart attack is reassured that his pains are only muscle spasms. Ewart's wife, Roz, calls in at the end of the shift. She has brought in his packed suitcase and their marriage is over.

EPISODE 3 — NIGHT RUNNERS
by Matthew Bardsley

Before stepping into the department, Baz has to certify a young black girl dead on arrival in the ambulance. Duffy is revising the Highway Code for her driving test. An innocent youth assaulted in a mugging is accused of attacking a policeman. He is later discharged from the hospital but soon returns when his deranged father threatens him with a Stanley knife, and also threatens the male staff. Clive is fed up with the racial prejudice of patients. A girl Christian Scientist refuses to sign a consent form for an emergency appendectomy. Megan asks everyone to pray for the girl, and her pain is miraculously relieved.

EPISODE 4 — JUMP START
by Susan Wilkins

Ewart is angry when he discovers Charlie has invited a Fleet Street journalist (Alfred Molina) to write about the permanent night shift. Tired of waiting, the reporter gets drunk and needs help from the staff to sober up. There's a motorway accident involving two men in a lorry and a couple in a car. The men survive but the couple die. The Medical Registrar is keen to extract organs from the woman. Two Madonna wanabees turn up, one with a bleeding nose after a DIY ear-piercing job went wrong. Kuba teaches Clive a lesson when he fills his whisky bottle with cold tea. A young black teenager seems drunk, but his behaviour results from head injuries and the team must operate.

EPISODE 5 — BLOOD BROTHERS
by Wally K Daly

An unhelpful newspaper article reveals nothing about the work of the department. It focuses on 'sexy' receptionists and 'nubile' doctors instead. A Samaritan is accused of assault when a young girl is beaten about the face after taking a paracetamol overdose. A ferret escapes from the care of a waiting patient and Susie is locked in the lavatory. A haemophiliac refuses a life-saving blood transfusion because of the fear of Aids. A transfusion is forced on him. A policeman panics when he gets blood on his hand, but Susie reassures him.

Ewart goes flat-hunting and Baz is offered another job.

EPISODE 6 — HIGH NOON
by Ray Brennan

During a lively meeting, chaired by NUPE shop steward Charlie, Duffy calls for a demonstration outside the local cinema which is showing 'naughty nurse' films. Baz sleeps with a doctor, an old friend, who has turned up in the department. A law student denies that he has had an epileptic fit and discharges himself. Charlie gives him a lift and advice as he walks from the hospital. The team has a Subbuteo contest in the staff room, and Ewart loses to an inexperienced Susie. At the cinema Duffy punches the Greek owner. She's arrested, with Megan, Susie and Kuba, but all are later discharged from the police station.

EPISODE 7 — PROFESSIONALS
by Susan Wilkins

A woman, raped and assaulted, comes in with her young son. Charlie discovers the boy has also been sexually abused. His architect father turns up and is interviewed by Charlie and Dr Claire (Stella Gonet). An alcoholic tramp infests the department with fleas, leaving the staff scratching for the rest of the shift. Ewart is dazzled by the glamorous boss of the new hospital cleaning company, but she outrages the A & E staff when she sacks a long-serving cleaner. Charlie and Baz spend the afternoon in bed after Charlie criticizes her for keeping herself awake on 'speed'. Megan discovers she has cervical cancer but can't tell husband Ted. She can talk it through with Ewart, though. At the end of a shift, there's a punch-up in reception and Duffy goes home with a split lip.

EPISODE 8 — CRAZIES
by Matthew Bardsley

Charlie finely tunes his car, ready for Duffy who is due to take a driving test at the end of the shift. Two taxi drivers are brought in when ammonia is thrown in their faces by a crazed woman. Their eyes are irrigated, but Megan is worried about the safety of her husband Ted, also a cabbie. The woman concerned gets into his taxi but he avoids her attack. Duffy's friend, Trish, also a Holby nurse and a part-time barmaid, is

Alfred Molina played a sneaky reporter in 'Jump Start'

sexually assaulted by a regular in the bar who has offered her a lift home. During the struggle, her fingers are trapped in the car door. Duffy has to treat them, making Trish shriek in pain. Ewart has a date with the cleaning firm boss. It's a flop! They disagree over Holby's cleaning policy. Megan has to spell out to Ted what her hysterectomy will mean. At the end of the shift, Duffy climbs into Charlie's car, but it won't start.

EPISODE 9 — MOONLIGHT BECOMES YOU
by Ray Brennan

Ambulance man Ponting has spent the night with Sandra Mute. They awake and she reminds him he's a married man. Clive and Charlie make fun of Duffy who has failed her driving test. An old man from a home is brought in. His four pals steal the home's minibus to travel to see him. They help him dress and shave to look his best for a lady friend but he dies before she arrives. An athletic young man complains of leg pain but he won't let any women investigate. In fact he has a boil on his bum. A drunk teenager is sick over Megan. She refuses to talk, then its discovered it's Ewart's daughter, Gillian. Ponting and Mute pick up a man who has crashed his car. He turns out to be an armed robber with a bullet in his chest. On their way to hospital, they are obstructed by a car full of jeering skinheads. They crash and one of the youths is brought in as well.

EPISODE 10 — TEENY POPPERS
by Janey Preger

Megan goes into hospital and is welcomed with balloons and her friends in A & E. An Asian boy gets drunk after breaking into a house with his mates. They attempt to revive him with pills; a blood vessel bursts and he dies in casualty. His mother and sister threaten Ewart with a lawsuit, saying he should have done more. Charlie, Clive and Kuba kidnap a bored Megan. She chats in the staff room to Ewart's daughter, there to visit her father. A man dressed as Spiderwoman, who has fallen off a balcony during a sexual fantasy, and a suicidal mum who hates her baby arrive. And a young boy almost persuades Duffy and Kuba to tend his sick dog.

EPISODE 11 — DRUNK
by Lise Meyer

Charlie chases Baz through an empty corridor and they kiss in the staff room. Baz then goes to see Megan, asleep after her operation. A restaurant owner chops off a finger. Mute retrieves it from a strawberry ice cream. Decorators are in as rumours fly of a royal visit. A school disco ends in disaster when a boy almost drowns in the school pool. The girl he fancies has stood him up. In crash, Baz shocks him back to life. Duffy is late for the night shift. She has been raped by a man she tried to help. She doesn't want to talk.

EPISODE 12 — QUIET
by Roy Mitchell

Duffy visits Megan in the ward and tells her about her attack, something she has been unable to talk about to others. A drunk (Sean Scanlon) pesters Susie. Ewart watches a local boxing tournament live on Kuba's TV. It ends in a knockout but it's the winner who's brought in after collapsing from a brain injury. Baz is unable to save an elderly alcoholic woman who dies in a pool of blood. A pregnant woman faces a Caesarean section. Baz, Ewart, Charlie and Clive battle to save the life of a heroin addict who needs a stomach wash-out. Ponting has a phone call at work – his wife has left him after finding a note from Sandra in his lunch box. What's big, white and missing? An ambulance, spotted speeding up the motorway.

EPISODE 13 — NO FUTURE
by Paul Unwin and Jeremy Brock

Megan, convalescing at home, is woken early by the police staging a siege next door. Her neighbour (Harold Goodwin), dying of cancer, has locked himself in his shed and says he has a child hostage. Megan talks him round. Baz gives herself a pregnancy test and avoids a suspicious Charlie. A Danish man dies in a crash. Ewart discovers he was a drug dealer. The man's female partner disappears, having failed to give her address. Ewart swiftly calls the police. Ironically, Kuba asks Charlie for advice on relationships. An old woman who has a crush on Charlie arrives and asks for a hug. He obliges. Megan's neighbour dies shortly after he tells her his cancer was caused by an atom bomb test he took part in after the war.

EPISODE 14 SURVIVAL
by Wally K Daly

Ewart's wife, Roz, asks him to meet her at the spot where he proposed to her. There she asks him to come back – he laughs at the idea. Charlie spots Baz arriving home with a male friend from an abortion clinic. She denies the rumours which spread fast but she does confess to Charlie. It would have been his

child. An old man collapses while Christmas shopping and is brought in. His daughter is one of the doctors but they don't get on with each other. There's a reconciliation of sorts. Ted tells Megan two passengers of his were hospital bosses who were talking about closing the night shift. Ewart later admits as much and the team decide to fight. Somehow, Clive and Ewart advise a young man, petrified about his sexual performance on his wedding night.

EPISODE 15 CLOSURE
by Jeremy Brock

The staff hear the bad news: they are to be shut down in one month. They meet to discuss ways of gaining public support. Kuba

breaks up a fight between a squabbling couple and brings the girl into casualty. He's scared he will be beaten up in revenge if he explains how the girl was injured. Ewart invites Kuba to spend the New Year with him for his own safety. A missionary is brought in with suspected Lassa fever. Charlie organizes an impromptu pantomime to raise morale. The axe falls on the department. Susie and Duffy stage a demonstration the following day.

Series 2—1987

EPISODE 1 A LITTLE LOBBYING
by Jeremy Brock and Paul Unwin

The night shift has closed and Holby A & E is open from nine to five only, with emergencies at other times going to the unit at Queen's Hospital. Elizabeth Straker, the new General Manager, and Ewart seem set to clash. A single parent has to travel twice as far to Queen's one night, when her toddler swallows sleeping pills. A young motorcyclist is killed when he is involved in a collision with a car. Ponting believes his life could have been saved if Holby's casualty had been open. Duffy applies for another nursing job and gets it. Baz has left Holby: she left Charlie a note. At a meeting at Megan's that evening, there's hope for the night shift, if they whip up support. They lobby, drop leaflets, and use the newspapers. Ewart makes a

Megan's husband Ted (Nigel Anthony), joins in the protest against closure

winning speech at the board meeting. There's a victory party at the pub. Duffy is lured back and Dr Mary Tomlinson asks Ewart if she can be his new Casualty Officer.

EPISODE **2** **A DROP OF THE HARD STUFF** *by Roy Mitchell*

The department has had a facelift and on the first night Charlie introduces student nurses Karen O'Malley and Cyril James. Dr Mary Tomlinson arrives too. Ewart invites Elizabeth Straker to shadow him for a shift. She's shocked at what they have to deal with. Mary discovers a young woman, desperate to be pregnant, who has been having sex through her urethra. The girl discharges herself but is brought in again after being hit by a drunk driver; she dies. An alcoholic stumbles into reception and a stabbed man is brought in. Duffy is horrified to find it's the man who raped her the previous year. She's not sorry he dies. Susie arranges an after-shift party. Charlie and Karen become close friends which irks Cyril. Elizabeth surprises Ewart by turning up.

EPISODE **3** **SHADES OF LOVE** *by Wally K Daly*

Charlie, on the rebound from Baz, spends the night with Karen. Cyril calls for her to play squash. When a man has a heart attack in the next court, they down raquets to resuscitate him. Susie falls for the new local bobby and Mary treats an elderly woman suffering from Alzheimer's disease. A woman is hit in a road accident by the wife of a man she's been having an affair with. In crash the wife tries to suffocate her, but is foiled by Megan. A model, Bunny Hopps, comes in and Mary suspects she has skin cancer. Ewart and Roz discuss divorce. Charlie explains to Karen that their night together was a one-off. She's upset.

EPISODE **4** **CRY FOR HELP** *by Jeremy Brock and Paul Unwin*

Ponting and Mute are called to help a Polish couple when the man suffers an electric shock. Two female Country and Western fans fight in reception over a man. Duffy's purse, containing £50, is stolen along with Ewart's Walkman. The thief turns out to be an attention-seeking old man, who is forced to return the belongings when Kuba and Ewart discover him in the loo. A suicidal medical student threatens to jump from the top of a tall building. A fellow student talks him down. As he's being driven to casualty, a drunk, already in the ambulance, stabs Mute in the stomach, flings open the rear doors and escapes. Ponting makes the student drive while he treats Mute. The team battles to save her but she dies.

EPISODE **5** **ANACONDA** *by Ray Brennan*

A dozy snake-charming artiste tells an audience of pensioners that one of her snakes has escaped. Everyone rushes to leave the club but many are injured and taken to casualty. Duffy and Susie are intrigued to learn that the artiste is a friend of straight-faced Dr Mary. A freelance photographer (Tony Selby) witnesses a brutal attack on an old Asian man and calls an ambulance. He photographs the attack and sends the results to a tabloid newspaper. When they are published, some youths are arrested. The photographer invites Susie to do a spot of modelling for him after he chats her up. Ewart invites Elizabeth Straker out to a restaurant, but he is delayed by a meeting with his lawyer about divorce. Elizabeth fumes. The entire team meets at the church for Sandra Mute's funeral.

EPISODE **6** **LIFELINES** *by Jeremy Brock*

A group of cavers go potholing in underground caves in Holby. The lone girl (Dee Sadler) suffers an epileptic fit while climbing a rope. She struggles and causes a rock to fall on a fellow crew member. Charlie is called out and almost slips down a crevice. Grieving Ponting works his final shift but there's a surprise party in the staff room for him. Ewart argues with Elizabeth over hospital security. Then she asks him out to dinner. Mary is unhappy about Duffy's work as acting Sister – she becomes deeply involved with a patient who later accuses Kuba of stealing his wallet. In fact the man left it in a taxi. Susie's modelling snaps are used without her consent.

EPISODE 7 — THE RAID
by Susan Wilkins

Shirley Franklin, one of the new ambulance team (with Keith Cotterill), has trouble getting to work when the police block off her street. Her son is missing and

Ella Wilder played paramedic Shirley Franklin after Sandra Mute died

she's worried. The police are aggressively questioning locals in her black community about drugs. A riot erupts in the night and Charlie and Mary are on standby as the injured are brought in. Once again, Duffy flaps under pressure as acting Sister, upsetting Megan and Susie. Megan's husband Ted crashes his taxi.

Shirley returns home to find the estate like a battlefield and her son safe and well in the care of a neighbour (Pam Ferris).

EPISODE 8 — CROSS FINGERS
by David Ashton

Cyril and Karen revise for their exams. Megan moonlights at a nursing home to earn extra cash. Duffy keeps quiet about Peter, her new boyfriend and the first since the rape. But Karen spills the beans after she spots them together. A heavy gambler becomes angry with his girlfriend when she won't go to a roulette game. She's feeling ill. When she changes her mind and calls a cab, the driver is Ted in a borrowed car. She collapses in pain and Ted drives her to the hospital. Dr Mary discovers she is suffering from meningitis, but it's caught in time. Charlie receives a letter – he has won £5,000 on the Premium Bonds.

EPISODE 9 — SEEKING HEAT
by Ray Brennan and Jeremy Brock

It's time for Ewart and Roz's divorce hearing. Ewart is left with nothing. Karen and Cyril pass their exams, but Karen reveals her plans to leave nursing and go to London. Ewart and Elizabeth continue their affair more openly. There's a massive explosion in a block of flats, caused by a couple on the ground floor making a bomb. Duffy's frosty relationship with Mary thaws when they are

called out together to assist at the bomb scene. Mary, accompanied by a fireman, scrambles through rubble to treat a young man found alive by a heat-seeking camera. They save him and rush him to casualty. An elderly woman, also injured in the blast, is brought in. Her son (Christopher Ellison) rails at Megan because she's Irish, and thus, he insists, responsible for the IRA. This upsets Megan immensely. Ewart provides a shoulder to cry on.

EPISODE 10 — ROCK A BYE BABY
by Ginnie Hole

Charlie considers buying a Cadillac with his winnings. Duffy's boyfriend Peter offers her an all-expenses paid trip to America. She refuses. An old woman is brought in by her daughter after falling from her commode. She needs a hip replacement. On seeing her suffering, Charlie thinks about spending his money on his mum, who also needs a new hip. He sees a Land Rover for £600 and snaps it up. A group of yelling skinheads disrupts the department, insulting Cyril. A teenage girl sniffs lighter fuel and is brought in only to collapse. Ewart has to tell her parents she has died. As the team leaves the next morning, Keith has to dash to his wife's side – she's in labour. But all goes well. A hopeful Karen gives Charlie her phone number in London.

EPISODE 11 HOOKED
by Billy Hamon

Peter breaks the news to Duffy that he is HIV positive. Later he leaves her a note at work to say he has left her. Duffy asks Mary if she should have an Aids test. Ted decides to move to Cheltenham where he can drive minicabs with his cousin. Megan is angry she was not consulted first. A male transvestite poses as a prostitute and picks up two young men. When they discover 'she's' male, they go to casualty and demand Aids tests. The prostitute's next customer has a heart attack and 'she' rushes to casualty with him. Her previous clients spot 'her', and beat 'her' up. A religious fanatic comes in – his penis is swollen. Charlie has decided to pay for his mum's operation. Elizabeth arrives at Megan and Ted's 25th wedding anniversary party. She invites Ewart for supper to meet her daughter.

EPISODE 12 FUN NIGHT
by Al Hunter

Duffy tries to track Peter down, because the police are unable to help her. Ted takes Megan to Cheltenham but she wants to stay in Holby with her friends. Susie goes to a punk concert where a fight breaks out. She drives a punk, who has a deep cut from a broken glass, to hospital. Two brothers are assaulted while walking home from the concert and one, suspected of seeing another man's girlfriend, is stabbed in the stomach. The other later dies in crash from his wounds. Ewart dines with Elizabeth and Louise, who tells him she's pregnant. Ewart advises an abortion, making Elizabeth angry. Cyril wins a bet that he could persuade antisocial Mary to have breakfast with him. Mary guesses it's a bet and chooses an expensive hotel. Kuba gives Susie a medal for bringing in the punk.

EPISODE 13 PEACE BROTHER
by David Ashton

Mary's parents are staying with her when her unemployed father collapses and is rushed to casualty. Ewart treats him when Mary finds herself unable to do so. The team are curious when Mary's boyfriend Brendan shows up. Duffy confides her worry about Peter to Susie. Susie tries to phone him but the line is dead. Ted tells Charlie that his plans to move to Cheltenham have fallen through. Megan admits that things aren't well between them. A rough countryman, with a huge tribe in tow, brings in his son, knocked unconscious during a fight between a landowner and trespassers. The boy needs X-rays and to be kept in for observation, so the tribe stays too.

EPISODE 14 BURNING CASES
by Jeremy Brock and Paul Unwin

A paraplegic locks himself in his bedroom and starts a fire, burning his hands in a moment of frustration. He is kept in hospital and his wife says that she will leave him unless he sorts himself out. An old woman with arthritis falls downstairs. She remains there until a neighbour spots her through the letterbox. Megan attends to her in a cubicle. As she goes to call a doctor, the woman falls from the trolley and later dies. The safety bar on the trolley was left down and Megan fears she will be blamed for her death. Ewart has a mild heart attack and is in hospital himself. Both his wife and Elizabeth arrive to see him. It's the first time they have met. Peter finally turns up to see Duffy. He's drunk and depressed. The virus has lost him his job.

EPISODE 15 THESE THINGS HAPPEN
by David Ashton

There's an internal investigation into the trolley fall death. Charlie helps Megan with her notes. The old woman's neighbour is brought in after an overdose but she survives. The dead woman's daughter insists it was negligence. Elizabeth visits Ewart who is recovering from his heart attack. Some girls are celebrating a birthday. A young male kiss-o-gram turns up. As they all leave the pub, a drunk driver ploughs into them. Charlie recognizes one of Holby's nurses under her blood-spattered clothes. The inquest and the investigation into the trolley death take all day. It's the next afternoon before Megan knows she has been cleared.

Series 3—1988

EPISODE 1 — WELCOME TO CASUALTY
by David Ashton

Cyril has been working in theatre at Queen's Hospital for six months and returns to Holby, applying for a full-time job in A & E. Charlie isn't keen, believing he should apply for something better. Megan is living alone in a high-rise flat. She sees her husband in Cheltenham every fortnight. One of Ewart's friends, a security guard on a building site, is brutally attacked and taken to casualty. He later manages to get his attackers arrested. Duffy's ex-boyfriend Peter dies in a car accident and his sister comes to Holby to break the news to Duffy.

While working at her father's garage, a young girl motor mechanic is trapped by a car, and new medic Dr David has to tell her she is paralysed from the neck down. A lorry driver comes in. Charlie knows he is a hopper (a persistent patient who hops from one hospital to another). He flees as soon as he's rumbled.

EPISODE 2 — DESPERATE ODDS
by Ginnie Hole

Ewart shows new manager Valerie around and learns that she has fixed Cyril's job. A social worker investigating the case of an abused child is assaulted by the angry stepdad. His condition is critical – he has a blood clot on the brain. The stepdad goes on to attack the young boy, who is constantly crying in his locked bedroom. The police arrive to stop him from beating the boy. A pickpocket, on remand with chest pains, is escorted into the department by two police officers. David believes he is faking but Cyril thinks he is telling the truth. He is discharged and taken back to the station. Keith and Shirley are later called out when he has a second stroke in the police cell. David blames himself when the man dies. A son brings in his elderly mother who has gangrene in her foot. Ewart explains that they must amputate it in the morning. The son indignantly asks for private care.

EPISODE 3 — DRAKE'S DRUM
by Keith Dewhurst

Student nurse, Alison McGrellis, spends a day with Keith and Shirley. Their first call is to a young asthmatic girl, whose breathing is made worse by her arguing parents. They also call on an old man with a rare heart condition. David suspects a cardiac tamponade and calls the Medical Registrar, who operates successfully in crash. The man's vicar (Julian Wadham) also arrives in casualty, with an itchy rash. Duffy gives him some cream. When he reveals he has Aids, Duffy advises him. Ewart takes a night boat trip with a colleague, and learns that Valerie may axe their observation ward. Valerie has been trying to contact him all evening about this. At midnight, a noisy argument ensues.

New nurse Cyril James (Eddie Nestor) worked hard for little thanks

EPISODE 4 — ABSOLUTION
by Wally K Daly

Valerie tells Ewart that the observation ward is to be closed. He says he'll fight. An old woman collapses at the airport on returning from Nigeria. Keith and Shirley believe she is suffering from malaria. She turns out to have thirty condoms full of heroin in her stomach and needs urgent treatment. Charlie notifies the police, against David's wishes. A Catholic woman confesses to her priest that she is pregnant by her brother-in-law. Later she cuts her wrists. Megan, who's Catholic, is asked to quiz the priest but tells Charlie her confession is confidential. In crash, the woman miscarries. Duffy thinks a patient is her Peter. She flees the cubicle, angering Charlie. Later she explains and they visit his grave. Megan has tension pains in her stomach. Is it cancer again? Ewart suggests tests. A woman who thinks she has breast cancer comes in. Her husband objects to male doctors seeing her, but the cancer worries are unfounded.

EPISODE 5 — BURN OUT
by Jeremy Brock

Megan's school teacher friend has pain from the facial plastic surgery needed after she was attacked by pupils. David diagnoses septicaemia. A young pregnant squatter is in labour and Keith delivers her baby girl in the ambulance. Ewart approaches the General Manager behind Valerie's back and wins back the observation ward. Megan has been heading towards a crisis. Suddenly in the middle of the shift she breaks down and screams at a complaining patient. Ewart sympathizes with her before visiting the observation ward. While there he has a second heart attack. Megan's mouth-to-mouth resuscitation fails. So do the efforts of the team in crash.

Administrator Valerie Sinclair (Susan Franklyn) seemed keen on Charlie

EPISODE 6 — A QUIET NIGHT
by David Ashton

Valerie arranges a service for Ewart at the hospital. A rugby player comes in with a broken nose, bleeding profusely. A sewerage worker who slipped and dislocated a shoulder comes in, as does a woman with a mysterious rash. It has been brought on by the death of her husband, whose body is still in the house. Cyril finds two of David's hockey sticks in the staff room. He and Charlie play with them in the corridor. David is furious, then challenges Cyril to a game. Two school minibuses, packed with pupils, collide on a country road. Cyril and David are called out while the team treats a stream of casualties. Charlie telephones all the parents.

EPISODE 7 — A WING AND A PRAYER
by Ginnie Hole

Student nurse Kiran Joghill's flat is burgled. She and Alison incur Charlie's anger when they're late for work because of it. Valerie is dining with boyfriend Michael when she's interrupted by Charlie, trying to sort out bed shortage problems. Megan becomes a grandmother. A middle-aged man (Roy Kinnear) suffers pains in his chest while playing snooker. In casualty, he is told his pains are caused by the poisonous fumes he has been inhaling at his poorly ventilated workplace. He's given the only available bed. Keith and Shirley are called out by an off-duty GP whose elderly patient has had a stroke. Keith explains that they cannot admit him. The GP writes a note to Dr David, stressing how sick his patient is. Kiran is angry when she learns that another patient has had the last bed. A baby is brought in dead – it's a cot-death.

EPISODE 8 · LIVING MEMORIES
by Sam Snape

Keith and Shirley bring in a young girl with breathing difficulties. Her mother (Pauline Quirke) is distraught until Duffy has good news of a recovery. Valerie conducts a 'customer survey' in the department, quizzing patients about their treatment. A teenage boy, involved in a road accident, suffers irreversible brain damage. His father won't agree to his organs being taken for transplant. His wife later changes his mind but by then it is too late. Alison and Kiran plan to move into Cyril's flat, but Kiran knows her strict Asian parents will not approve. Two charity fund-raisers, in fancy dress, are brought in drunk, disorderly and, when they sober up, guilt-ridden.

EPISODE 9 · INFERNO
by Ginnie Hole

It's bonfire night, a nightmare for the team. An inaccurate meningitis scare story appears in the press. A child with head pains is brought in and meningitis is diagnosed. A hairdresser, suffering from chronic PMT, has a blazing row with her husband in which she accidentally cuts her wrist with a breadknife. The department is full of children with firework burns. Valerie is a guest at a private firework display, which is gatecrashed by a group of children. They steal rockets and

throw them into the bonfire, setting off other fireworks. During the rumpus a small boy falls into the fire and suffers third-degree burns. Valerie burns her hands and is treated by Charlie. Charlie invites her for coffee. The department has got to make economies – Charlie must sack either Megan or Kuba.

EPISODE 10 · CARING
by Jeremy Brock

A leukaemia victim takes an overdose during the final weeks of his life. Duffy comforts his wife. David wants her to see the Psychiatric Registrar. A man is brought in by his brother (Clive Mantle, who now plays Dr Mike Barratt). He has been vomiting blood, because of an arthritis drug prescribed by his GP. The man dies and David discovers the GP is their own new locum Medical Registrar, Dr Roth. A retired couple, both former doctors, arrive. The woman has collapsed after keeping her cancer symptoms from her husband. Charlie courageously invites Valerie to dinner. She accepts.

Series 4—1989

EPISODE 1 · CHAIN REACTION
by Ginnie Hole

A leather-clad motorcyclist arrives in A & E and unzips. It's Alex Spencer, a new student nurse. Newly-promoted Sister Duffy is

not amused. Dr Lucy Perry treats a young woman with advanced cervical cancer before being called out with Cyril to a road crash. A car has collided with a lorry carrying drums of chemicals and a second car has spun over. A young girl hitchhiker, trying to resist a sexual advance, was thrown through the car windscreen and has head injuries, and the driver has a ruptured spleen. The lorry driver (Pat Roach) needs a chest drain which Dr Perry performs on the side of the road. A policeman is burned when he falls into a pool of acid. Back in casualty, he dies just as his young wife arrives to visit him.

EPISODE 2 · ACCIDENTS HAPPEN
by Bill Gallagher

A housewife trips on her vacuum cleaner cable, falls downstairs and is found unconscious by her neighbour, a mentally handicapped youth. In casualty, her husband (Colin Baker) angrily accuses the boy of causing the accident. Registrar Dr Andrew Bower, who's going out with Duffy, operates to remove a blood clot on the brain. Cyril applies for a job in Intensive Therapy but is unlucky. Duffy finds out the cause of a pensioner's neck wound – his dog bit him but the old man doesn't want the dog destroyed. Cyril stitches an American woman's gashed forehead. She tells him of the nursing opportunities in the USA. He's tempted.

EPISODE 3 A GRAND IN THE HAND
by Sam Snape

Four young people are celebrating as they travel in a beaten-up yellow Mini. A suicidal woman driving a sturdy Volvo estate recklessly crashes into them. Two die instantly and a girl dies in casualty. A policeman who has spotted cans of lager in the wrecked Mini wants to breathalyze the young driver who has a serious head injury, but Dr Andrew and Charlie know that could be fatal. Later the driver's sister prompts the Volvo driver to admit it was her fault. On a building site, a worker (Joe McGann) slips and hot bitumen spills onto him and he falls from the scaffolding. In casualty, his boss tries to buy his silence with £1,000 but his wife (Shirin Taylor) won't allow it. Charlie finds Megan stealing Valium and makes her flush her supply away. Alex soothes a child worried about a pet chicken.

 ## EPISODE 4 DAY OFF
by Jacqueline Holborough

In the pub at lunchtime, hospital porter Jimmy finds the pub comedian in the toilets, stabbed. He needs a chest drain. The police suspect Jimmy but the culprit is a deranged young man who has killed his flatmate and also slashed his own wrists. Alex gives a patient a painkiller before a doctor sees him. Duffy snaps at her. It's the day she has found out

she's pregnant. Dr Andrew is discussing a new posting and Duffy tells him she'll have the baby on her own and she doesn't love him. But new receptionist Julie agrees to go out with Jimmy.

EPISODE 5 VITAL SPARK
by John Fletcher

An old poacher patiently shows his grandson his favourite haunts. Later that day he collapses. The boy drives him to casualty where he dies peacefully. A monk, who fears he has lost his faith, tries to hang himself. When he is brought in Duffy preaches to him before it's discovered he has also tortured himself with a studded belt. Lucy talks about art to a dreamy housewife who has ruptured herself trying to do exotic dancing. And a seventy-eight-year-old with VD reveals he caught it from the Meals on Wheels lady.

EPISODE 6 CHARITY
by Margaret Phelan

A child in a caravan is choking from asthma. Her father tries to bring her into casualty. First his car breaks down, then the parked cars belonging to guests at a hospital charity do block the path of the ambulance. Stretchered in, the little girl dies in crash. An elderly man with a thrombosis still manages to mistreat his helpless wife. Lucy copes with a woman's ectopic pregnancy and a young man at the charity party,

Cheery nurse Alex Spencer (Belinda Davison) drove a motorbike fast and drove Duffy mad

who has had a stroke. An elderly woman with cancer is left in the corridor because there's no bed for her. Alex curses a man who gropes her and is told off by Duffy. But she's cheered when she grabs the stomach of a patient who has swallowed a tooth, to make him cough it up.

EPISODE 7 VICTIM OF CIRCUMSTANCE
by Ginnie Hole

An Asian schoolboy is beaten up while delivering newspapers from his dad's shop. The team is horrified to learn that all the family have been victims of racist thugs. Later they attack again. The seven-year-old son of a single actress mum is brought in by his teacher. He may have appendicitis. As Lucy waits for his mother to arrive, Duffy thinks about her own pregnancy. A carpenter (Tim Healy) who has waited a year for a heart by-pass collapses at work. He's brought in and Alex later finds he has died in a cubicle. Charlie learns that Queen's, not Holby, is to have a new trauma centre.

DELUGE
by Bill Gallagher

Charlie tackles Valerie about the bed shortage which means patients, including a woman who has miscarried, are parked in the corridor. At a garden centre reception, the owner's young daughter gets drunk and needs her stomach pumped. Jimmy also got drunk while out with Julie and it takes the whole shift before she accepts his apology. A teenage boy has swallowed a tooth knocked out in a boxing ring. It's lodged in a lung and he needs an operation. Alex, out with the paramedics, coaxes a timid old woman with an arm injury into casualty. A madman comes in, shouting abuse and banging his head on the reception desk, leaving the old lady cowering in fright.

UNION
by Jacqueline Holborough

Megan has talked to reporters about the staff and bed shortage and faces a disciplinary hearing. There are agency nurses today because Charlie is away on a course and Duffy's in charge. A

twelve-year-old Sudanese girl is brought in seriously ill after her grandmother circumcised her. She dies and Lucy tells the family the practice is illegal. Alex is distressed by this and Jimmy comforts her. Seeing them, Duffy gets the wrong idea. Later the Surgical Consultant sees Lucy demonstrating relaxation techniques to an anxious man. He warns her that her 'new fangled' ideas aren't acceptable.

TAKING STOCK
by Barry Purchese

A couple argue as they prepare to auction their bankrupt farm. When the wife says the marriage is over, her husband taunts her and she shoots him. He forgives her in the ambulance then dies in crash. A working mother finds her two-year-old son with an aspirin bottle. She becomes hysterical when he has to have a blood test. Receptionist Julie could be in trouble for giving confidential information to the police about a mugger. The man and his female victim, who sprayed his eyes with mace, come together in casualty. Lucy is shunned by the Surgical Registrar and given the job of removing a shield with KY jelly from the swollen arm of a man in full Viking costume.

BANKING FOR
BEGINNERS
by Bryan Elsley

Alex lunches with a boyfriend

who offers her a well-paid job in banking. Between courses she resuscitates a heart attack victim. An old lady (Patricia Hayes) is brought in with a broken hip. Jimmy suspects her daughter has pushed her downstairs. Lucy dismisses the idea, believing the old woman is senile. Later they find the daughter is the demented one. Val too ignores signs that an elderly woman neighbour needs help. She is brought in, suffering from hypothermia and later has a cardiac arrest. Val dithers over her report proposing staffing cuts yet it must go through. Lucy doesn't tell a footballer his playing days are over but his girlfriend does.

HANGING ON
by Sam Snape

At her leaving party Alex is drinking champagne from a bedpan. Then there's an explosion in the city centre. Two surgeons arrive to assist the team who treat a stream of stunned and injured people including a schoolgirl with a mangled foot and head wounds, a woman who has lost a hand and another with fragments of glass in her face. A shop assistant carries in a customer, not realizing she is dead. A baby is brought in – its mother is dead. Cyril discovers one patient is a shoplifter because her bag is full of jewellery. A reporter poses as a doctor until she's thrown out. Jimmy waits with the bodies. Under a sheet, a portable phone rings. He tells the worried wife he'll get her husband to call back.

EPISODE 1
PENALTY
by Ginnie Hole

A riot starts at a football game when an away supporter loses his ticket and watches the game from the home stand. It means a hectic first day for new staff, Registrar Dr Julian Chapman, Junior Houseman Dr Beth Ramanee and Staff Nurse Martin Ashford. One girl needs an emergency tracheotomy and Julian discovers she has a crushed spine. A family outing ends tragically. A young boy's mother is trampled to death in the mayhem. Megan hears about the football disaster on her radio – she arrives late. She had been burying her husband Ted. Paramedic Keith's day is better. He delivers twins.

EPISODE 2
RESULTS
by Ben Aaronovitch

It's a night for young casualties. A drug addict steals the supplies of paramedics Jane and Josh to experiment with his girlfriend (Linda Davidson). A brilliant student dies, poisoned by alcohol after celebrating success in his exams. A careering juggernaut throws a man through a shop window. He dies in crash. His widow attacks Megan. Duffy's son tires her. Charlie is depressed to find that his pal, who was nursing a broken leg, collapsed and died in an orthopaedic ward.

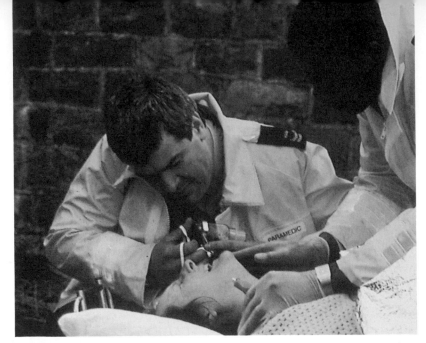

Shirley Franklin's ambulance partner was Keith Cotterill played by Geoffrey Leesley

EPISODE 3
CLOSE TO HOME
by Jim Hill

Charlie is low and Julian is tactless. But Megan is charmed by social worker Tony Walker who saves her as she's attacked by a neighbour (Melanie Kilburn) who is neglecting her small son. An injured fireman needs help. And Jimmy spends most of the shift looking for a stolen briefcase belonging to an old man. When he does find it, he's surprised that it contains women's clothes.

EPISODE 4
STREET LIFE
by Ian Briggs

Duffy spots hepatitis B symptoms in a prostitute with human bite marks on her leg. The woman won't stay but is later brought in, dead, after being badly beaten.

Megan worries about two homeless teenage girls, one stabbed in the arm by derelicts and seriously ill from a paracetamol overdose. Other 'customers' are a tyrannical old mother; a skinhead with a sex-mad girlfriend; and a heart patient's husband who's sicker than his wife.

EPISODE 5
HIDING PLACE
by Tony Etchells

An ex-boxer (John Bardon) uses his old skills on hooligans on a bus and ends up with two broken ribs. Beth clashes with Julian over his harsh treatment of a drug addict. A known hoaxer poses as a doctor to steal tranquillisers. And Tony Walker tempts Megan with a trip to Paris. When Ash tells her the man's married, she says she already knows.

EPISODE 6 — SALVATION
by Robin Mukherjee

A girl's legs are crushed when a group of yuppies race flash cars on a dark country road. A father's religious sect opposes dialysis for his child despite the pleas of her mother (Louise Jameson) and Julian's anger. Finally the father relents. A drunk, a diabetic and a heart attack victim all need mattresses in the corridor. A patient turns out to be the driver who almost ran Duffy down earlier. She spots his real problem – a brain tumour.

EPISODE 7 — SAY IT WITH FLOWERS
by Rona Munro

Stumbling on her stilettos, one of two model sisters dressed as chocolates for a sales promotion (Carol and Amanda Royle) ends up in casualty. So does a girl assaulted by a minicab driver (Mark McGann). Duffy draws on her own rape experience to advise her. An old woman collapses in the street and Megan and Beth discover she's carrying several thousand pounds in her handbag. Megan spells out to Charlie the risks of his current heavy drinking when he brings in his drinking companion who has cut a wrist on a broken glass.

EPISODE 8 — LOVE'S A PAIN
by Sam Snape

A doting grandfather (Denis Lill) climbs a ladder to retrieve a frisbee from the roof. He topples backwards, crushing the boy. In crash, the boy cannot be revived. But Julian's skill saves a knifed taxi driver, whose warring mother and teenage daughter make peace in the crisis. Police arrest a patient after his wife's lover, whom he attacked, dies of a brain haemorrhage. Duffy finds being a single mum is hard. Let down by a baby minder, she has to bring baby Peter to work.

EPISODE 9 — A WILL TO DIE
by Christopher Penfold

A man secretly meets his wife's best friend for love on a canal barge but after an explosion caused by a gas leak she's horrifically burned. An anorexic girl comes in with her bossy mother but overdoses and dies. Beth treats a young remand prisoner who has been beaten up and, she finds, raped. A well-dressed woman visits a patient, a drunken tramp. He's her son. Duffy's child-minding problems continue and so does Megan and Tony's affair.

EPISODE 10 — BIG BOYS DON'T CRY
by Ginnie Hole

Paramedics Josh and Lily find an elderly patient already dead and his crazed son menacing them with a butcher's knife. Later he threatens Jimmy in the same way. The team battle and save a schoolboy who tried to hang himself at school after weeks of being bullied. And Beth argues and proves to the paediatrician (Tessa Peake Jones) that a Greek couple's bruised baby is not battered but has brittle bones. Tony Walker's a womaniser, his wife tells Megan.

EPISODE 11 — REMEMBRANCE
by Robin Mukherjee

Jimmy's latest girlfriend, a student nurse, is brought in after a night of drink and drug-taking. Jimmy is suspended after she lies to Julian that he stole the drugs for her. A racist warehouse foreman and a worker arrive, ill from inhaling chlorine fumes after a cleaning fluid spillage, but alive thanks to their Sri Lankan skivvy. A man brings in his difficult mother-in-law (Jean Anderson) and asks Julian to end her life. Megan finds an ESN woman is about to give birth.

EPISODE 12 — ALL'S FAIR
by Stephen Wyatt

A teenage girl won't say why she tried to kill herself but her older sister (Louise Lombard) tells Megan that their widowed father has been sexually abusing the girl as he had earlier abused her. Julian's weekend 'war games' are halted when he has to turn up in casualty in camouflage with his partner who has injured an ankle tumbling from a rope bridge. Diabetic Ash is able to help a fellow sufferer and Duffy considers joining a nursing agency.

EPISODE 13 — A REASONABLE MAN
by Barbara Machin

A schizophrenic man (Kenneth Cranham) arrives after a road accident and, it transpires, his murder of his wife's friend. He panics at the sight of a policeman, pulls a gun from his briefcase, takes Megan hostage in crash and taunts her with his nightmares of betrayal. He insists that a porter (Charlie in Jimmy's uniform) removes a body that is already there. Megan stays calm but the police and the man's wife's shouts make him panic and fire, wounding Charlie in the chest.

Series 6 — 1991

EPISODE 1 — HUMPTY DUMPTY
by Ginnie Hole

Young outward-bounders, one ill from the cold, foolishly tackle a sheer rock face and fall to a cliff base. Julian and Duffy are winched to the rescue by helicopter and Julian performs an emergency amputation on one boy's foot. Jane abseils down to help the other victim. Back at Holby, Beth respects a dying cancer sufferer's wishes not to prolong his life. His daughter arrives after he dies, and accuses her father's partner of murder and Beth of negligence. Jimmy tries to chat up pretty blonde Kelly Liddle, who is beginning a six-month stint as a student nurse.

EPISODE 2 — JUDGEMENT DAY
by Barbara Machin

Beth faces the inquest on the cancer patient she didn't resuscitate. No negligence is found but the dead man's daughter threatens to sue privately. Jimmy, moonlighting on a market stall, brings into casualty a child burned when her tracksuit touched a portable gas fire. An athletics coach (Tom Georgeson) brings in his star sprinter, who has a sprained ankle and palpitations. It seems they fear a random drugs test but the girl's pills turn out to be harmless. A policewoman collapses. The cause, Duffy finds, is a retained tampon.

EPISODE 3 — DANGEROUS GAMES
by Robin Mukherjee

Julian hears on the grapevine that he has a chance of getting the consultant's job. Charlie likes social worker Trish Baynes when they meet at a bereavement counselling session. The team helps a young man and a young runaway girl suffering from carbon monoxide poisoning from a leaky heater. A young man, who has almost drowned in a swimming pool trying to impress a girl, is rushed in. Kelly comforts a shoplifter only to learn later that her baby died as a result of her neglect and mistreatment. A child is patched up after tumbling from a playground slide but her father has an epileptic fit when he visits her.

EPISODE 4 — HIDE AND SEEK
by David Richard-Fox

While Julian worries about competition for the consultancy, Jimmy chases a snake which has slithered from a patient's bag. Two children, one an asthmatic badgered by his father, are rushed in after being trapped in a fridge which was dumped by the other child's scrapdealer father. Kelly allows Jimmy to practise first aid on her, incurring Duffy's disapproval. And a heavy-drinking antiques dealer dies after a massive haemorrhage which covers Beth in blood. Kelly and Ash tie Jimmy into a strait-jacket only to incur Julian's displeasure at their prank.

EPISODE 5 — JOY RIDE
by Bill Gallagher

Three teenagers, the worse for drink, play traffic-light jumping in a stolen car. They crash, and one is hurled through the windscreen and dies in crash. One is badly injured, the third faces the police at Holby. A bride-to-be arrives with the two fingers she just lost at work in an abattoir. They can be stitched back. A neurotic wife (Polly James) confesses to Trish that her real problem is her husband's need for sex. A workaholic almost blinded by molten plastic and a gambler with memory loss who may have killed also come in. Kelly is over-keen to give a tetanus jab — something she's not allowed to do.

EPISODE 6 — SOMETHING TO HIDE
by Stephen Wyatt

A car bomb planted by Animal Rights activists causes chaos in a suburban street. An injured girl reveals she is the bomber when she shows distress that a victim is not the scientist who was targeted. Kelly and Duffy argue over her right to confidentiality. Charlie urges a teacher beaten up after cruising in a gay area to tell the police. He daren't. Beth suspects MS in a young man and two members of receptionist Norma's am-dram group arrive, dramatically. The show's star has hurt an ankle.

EPISODE 7 — BEGGARS CAN'T BE CHOOSERS
by Ginnie Hole

A man suffering from a severe kidney complaint is refused a bed by the Medical Registrar, to Beth's annoyance. He is rushed back to casualty hours later when septicaemia is diagnosed. A teenage drug addict is brought in after injecting temazepam. His supplier turns out to be his old aunt (Edna Dore), who believed the pills were harmless because her GP prescribed them for her. Julian advises the boy's parents about the risks of hepatitis and Aids and the father attacks the old aunt. Beth hears that the negligence suit is being dropped. She breaks down in Charlie's presence. Kelly upsets Duffy yet again by being late at the beginning of her shift.

EPISODE 8 — LIVING IN HOPE
by Robin Mukherjee

Julian celebrates landing the consultant's job while Duffy's boyfriend Paul Slater pressures her to leave nursing. A young woman riding her bike along a narrow lane collides with a heavy goods lorry. The team cannot save one of her legs. Two student back-packers return from holiday with heroin smuggled in swallowed condoms. The boy

Nurse Kelly Liddle (Adie Allen) couldn't cope

collapses and is saved in casualty. The girl dies in the loo after trying to vomit. Ash is punched and insulted in reception when he tries to settle an argument between a youth and his girlfriend. Duffy and Charlie warn Kelly about her lax attitude.

EPISODE 9 — MAKING THE BREAK
by Jacqueline Holborough

An old drunk (Jimmy Jewel) upsets the Holby medics after he injures a leg falling down the pub steps. His other leg is wooden. Trish is involved with a boy with human bite marks on his leg. It's the result of a human 'dog fight' that his father's friend forced him to take part in. Two nuns arrive, one with a fractured nose after the other hit her with a pudding spoon in the convent kitchen. A young blind girl is hit by a messenger riding a bike on the pavement: she regains her sight. Kelly takes a cocktail of pills and vodka.

EPISODE 10 — SINS OF OMISSION
by Bryan Elsley

The team is devastated by the news of Kelly's suicide. Duffy blames herself for being too critical. An elderly patient with a heart condition (Peggy Mount) arrives and is cheery in a cubicle but suddenly has a seizure and dies. Ash feels responsible. Jimmy befriends a vagabond who is living in the hospital basement, posing as a porter at mealtimes. A kit-car designer with money problems takes an insurance man on a test run in his new prototype car. It crashes. He suffers a broken leg but his passenger has multiple injuries.

EPISODE 11 — THE LAST WORD
by Barbara Machin

The team is relieved to welcome experienced staff nurse Sandra Nicholl, back at work after having a daughter, Laura. Both Jimmy and Julian are attracted to her. Sandra is presented with a problem she didn't have a few years earlier: a woman with a bleeding forehead who is HIV positive. A ballet dancer arrives with rectal bleeding. Ash learns of her efforts to remain slim – her diet consists of tissues and laxatives. Duffy refuses to quit nursing and her relationship with Paul ends.

 EPISODE 12 **PRESSURE? WHAT PRESSURE?**
by Arthur McKenzie

A woman with self-inflicted cigarette burns discharges herself but goes home only to be beaten up by her husband. She has violent abdominal pains as a result and on a second visit to casualty Beth diagnoses ectopic pregnancy. Beth is enraged by the woman's husband and slaps him across the face in the interview room. An obese man with a sprained ankle pleads to have his jaw wired to stop his over-eating. Two young men try glue-sniffing. One dies and Charlie and Julian clash over the ethics of organ donation.

 EPISODE 13 **FACING UP**
by Bill Gallagher

A young boy finds his father's loaded revolver and shoots his grandmother, who later dies in crash from the wound. Paramedics Josh and Jane have trouble enticing into the ambulance a mentally ill man

who has spilled hot fat over himself. A retired gardener (Geoffrey Bayldon) dislocates a rival gardener's jaw after he suspects him of ruining his prize leeks. Trish is attacked in her own office by an angry client whom she's powerless to help. She feels she must move on. Ash is visited by his sister who has rowed with their mother. Beth has an interview for a GP's job and finds that racism is alive and well.

EPISODE 14 **ALLEGIANCE**
by David Richard-Fox

A tabloid photographer crashes through the glass conservatory roof of a womanizing MP (Simon Shepherd) to snatch a photo. The MP's wife is crushed and the two men end up fighting in casualty. A middle-aged gay businessman (Frank Windsor) faces life without his partner who has suffered a fatal heart attack. The partner's daughter turns up, making her hostility to their lifestyle clear. An ageing rock guitarist (Brian Hibbard) electrocutes himself on an amplifier. His injuries are slight but his career is over. Beth gets her GP's job.

EPISODE 15 **CASCADE**
by Ginnie Hole

Horror strikes at Holby airport when a plane full of holiday-makers returning from Greece crashes into an embankment. The team is off-duty enjoying Beth's

leaving party but are soon on red alert to help the victims. Julian and Ash assist at the scene with cases including a man and a seven-year-old girl trapped in the cabin. Back at base, Beth, Charlie and Duffy deal with casualties through the night. One is the co-pilot, crushed by the controls. Charlie and Duffy ponder Holby's future as a trust hospital.

Series 7 — 1992/93

EPISODE 1 **RATES OF EXCHANGE**
by Barbara Machin

Two young men are injured when their car overturns, swerving to avoid a lorry. The driver dies and his parents (Julia Foster and Roshan Seth) have different opinions about organ donation. Nervous new SHO Dr Rob Khalefa nearly kills the injured passenger, by failing to insert a second drip. Ash takes pity on a homeless teenage girl who has slit her wrists. Her mother turns out to be a well-known prostitute in Holby. And cheeky Max, the new Health Care Assistant, falls foul of Duffy when she wears a bum-bag and chews gum in the department.

EPISODE 2 **CRY WOLF**
by David Richard-Fox

Seconds after an accident involving a young lad on a motorbike, off-duty paramedic Josh arrives at the scene. While

Josh calls for help, an interfering GP removes the boy's crash helmet, putting his spinal cord at risk. Holby's General Manager, Kate Miller, shadows a shift in the department. A toddler needs his stomach pumped after swallowing the cannabis which his father left lying around. Sandra believes she spots an attention-seeker but Julian discovers the patient's real problem is an obstructed bowel. By then she has fled. She is later brought back after collapsing.

General Manager Kate Miller (Joanna Foster) isn't tough enough for her boss

EPISODE 3 — BODY POLITIC
by Ginnie Hole

A teenage girl is brought in by her anxious mother (Jan Harvey), unaware her daughter is pregnant.

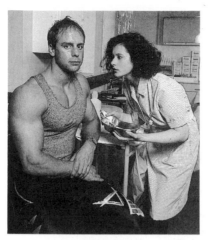

Little Maxine Price comforts a big body builder in 'Body Politic'

The girl confesses to Max that she has tried to end the pregnancy with a knitting needle. It slowly becomes clear that the mother's boyfriend has abused her repeatedly. An aristocrat is shot when a leather-clad biker with a crossbow calls on him. No surgeons are free and Julian is forced to operate to remove the bolt. He saves the man. The attacker turns out to be the mother of a child that the aristocrat killed on the road eight years before. Max discovers a collapsed body-builder in the hospital grounds. He is rushed into crash where he dies after Ash and Rob find steroids in his wallet. Norma worries about her mother, who has Alzheimer's disease.

EPISODE 4 — WILL YOU STILL LOVE ME?
by Helen Greaves

A young boy, frightened into silence by his mother's affair, is brought in with a sore throat. He later collapses outside casualty and dies in crash. Julian breaks the news to his mother and her lover (Jesse Birdsall). Ash faces financial troubles with live-in girlfriend Nikki. An unhappy old woman (Eleanor Summerfield) claims the staff at her nursing home have beaten her. She shows Duffy leg bruises, which are found to be self-inflicted. Her son must face up to living with her again. A teenage girl injured in a road accident suffers anew when a mental patient, posing as a doctor, sexually assaults her. Her overbearing father makes matters worse.

EPISODE 5 — CHERISH
by Catherine Johnson

A pregnant young Asian woman throws herself downstairs in an attempt to kill the unborn child she believes is female – not what her husband wants. She merely sprains a wrist. In Holby she retreats to the loo where hours later Julian and Sandra deliver a healthy baby son. Charlie treats a teenage boy, injured in a road accident. On unbuttoning 'his' shirt, it's clear this is a girl. A day's shopping brings two elderly sisters to casualty. One (Dora Bryan) steals a box of chocolates and fakes a collapse in order to dodge a store detective. The other proves to be seriously ill when a damaged leg leads to a fuller examination. Norma's mother wanders into reception and doesn't recognize her daughter.

PROFIT AND LOSS
by Stephen Wyatt

Max arranges a karaoke evening to boost hospital funds. Julian performs 'A Hard Day's Night' with Sandra. A family printing business goes up in smoke. Unknown to the owner (Michael Jayston), who has fixed the fire for an insurance fiddle, his son has returned there and is severely burned. A suicidal couple (Helen Lederer and Peter Gilmore) take a concoction of drugs. The man, who is terminally ill with Motor Neurone Disease, dies at their home but the woman is saved in time. An Asian man is brutally attacked and tells Duffy of the racial abuse his whole family endure. Smarmy General Manager, Simon Eastman, turns up to add to the pressures.

EPISODE
7
ONE STEP FORWARD
by Peter Bowker

A tea dance ends in a sprained ankle for one pensioner (Lionel Jeffries) when he rides his bicycle into his friend (Leslie Randall) whom he accuses of match-making with an old flame (Madge Ryan). A mentally handicapped girl who has failed to take her tranquillisers runs amok in the place. A squash game ends abruptly when a young woman accidentally smashes her raquet in two, slips and stabs herself in the neck with the handle. Julian has to perform emergency surgery. Max lets

slip her secret interest, the Territorial Army. Norma reaches the end of her tether with her mother.

EPISODE
8
BODY AND SOUL
by Peter Bowker

Duffy gives advice and support to a woman raped by her ex-husband. The woman is in trouble with another man, a too-friendly stranger on a railway platform into whose face she jabs her keys. Meanwhile, Duffy jumps the waiting list for a cervical biopsy, thanks to Julian pulling strings. At a fox hunt a saboteur is struck by a horse and dies in casualty. The horse is also killed. Its rider (Tenniel Evans) suffers a broken arm. Paramedic Jane spends the day observing the doctors at work. Simon transfers 'disobedient' Kate. Sandra's and Julian's affair finally begins.

EPISODE
9
TENDER LOVING CARE
by Barbara Machin

Duffy nervously awaits her test results. An old fusspot (Harry Towb) with angina collapses in his synagogue and is calmed in casualty. His more seriously ill wife (Maxine Audley) collapses with a leaking aortic aneurysm while with him. Julian is unable to resuscitate her. An unhappy student collapses on a field trip. When he's brought in, battling for his life, he admits he has sickle-cell anaemia. An unpleasant asthmatic who has not taken his

medication has an acute attack. At a busy time Rob examines him, then leaves a protesting Sandra to set up an intravenous penicillin drip. Max fails to pass on the fact that the man is allergic to penicillin.

EPISODE
10
MONEY TALKS
by Bryan Elsley

An electricity worker, on the day before he retires, falls from a pylon trying to rescue a birds' egg collector. He is taken to casualty where his wife (Marcia Warren) blames his boss. Rob denies he instructed Sandra to inject the asthmatic who has complained. She's in trouble. A young drugs dealer arranges a rave which his teenage sister attends. When she collapses he rushes her in, claiming she has alcohol poisoning. Rob accepts his story but Sandra suspects it's drugs and seeks Julian's opinion. Sandra tackles the brother who finally confesses to their mother that the girl has taken Ecstasy. The team manages to save her. Sandra visits Julian at home and prescribes bed.

EPISODE
11
MAKING WAVES
by Robin Mukherjee

It's Rob's day off, and he takes a private boat trip with girlfriend Natasha, and his father's friend, Bart (Martin Jarvis) and his wife (Rosalind Ayres). The boat hits choppy waters and crashes into a sand bank under Bart's mishandling. Rob tries to save

Mean and smarmy – we miss administrator Simon Eastman (Robert Dawe)

Natasha, who is swept away by the waves. Gibbering wreck Bart and his wife are rescued and taken to Holby. Later Natasha is resuscitated. Rob cracks under the pressure and admits to Julian that he's finding it hard to cope. A young drug addict is trying to kick her habit. Her boyfriend, who is HIV positive, visits. He needs her – to stay a junkie. Simon Eastman hears Rob's side of the complaint against Sandra. Duffy's cancer test is negative.

EPISODE 12 IF IT ISN'T HURTING
by Jacqueline Holborough

Sandra receives a written warning and she's furious. A farm owner (Philip Whitchurch) facing bankruptcy goes berserk and stages a siege. It ends in horror when he shoots dead his baby daughter and wounds himself and his son. His distraught wife learns in casualty that the boy remains critical. Ash and Nikki split up. A

cantankerous, disabled man (Philip Madoc) falls from his wheelchair and cuts his wrist. His wife takes him to casualty and tries to abandon him there. Duffy treats a traffic warden who, on her first day, has had her earring torn out of her ear by an abusive lorry driver.

EPISODE 13 ACT OF FAITH
by Catherine Johnson

Julian urges Sandra to leave her husband for him but she can't decide. Later he takes her daughter Laura to a circus. It's lucky he's in the audience to help. Not only does the dwarf knife-thrower (Kenny Baker, who played R2D2 in Star Wars) have an eye infection but the owner (Rula Lenska) has clashed with her trapeze artist son about new routines. Unrehearsed he goes ahead and his pretty partner falls, seriously injuring herself. Back at base, Julian's affair with Sandra becomes clear. Another patient is a surrogate mother, beaten by her husband. She has decided to keep the baby, leaving the childless wife (Susan Penhaligon) and her husband dismayed. Duffy is in touch with old boyfriend Andrew.

EPISODE 14 POINT OF PRINCIPLE
by Peter Bowker

An unemployed cycling enthusiast is racing a rival down a country road when their pedals lock and they collide at speed. He is taken to crash where Julian tries to

repair his damaged pelvis and leg. An ice skater, pushed by her father to compete relentlessly, deliberately lets a wheel of their car crush her foot. It means she's free. The owner of a pit bull terrier comes in with horrific gashes caused during a fight between two dogs. Julian later learns that Holby has failed in its bid to be granted a modern trauma unit and that his views were ignored by General Manager Simon Eastman. Enraged, he tells waiting reporters that he'll resign. Charlie tries to persuade him to retract and Sandra is saddened but says she won't leave her family for him. Julian speeds off in his Mercedes.

EPISODE 15 SILENT NIGHT
by Ginnie Hole

The team goes for a Christmas meal at an Indian restaurant before the night shift. A battered middle class wife (Dorothy Tutin) is preparing a large turkey but her son (Jeff Rawle) says his family won't be coming. Her husband (TP McKenna) taunts her and she stabs him. Josh and Jane bring the couple in but a young homeless girl Rob has discharged runs in front of the ambulance, causing it to swerve and hit a lamp post. The stabbed man dies, Jane has whiplash injuries and the girl breaks a leg and arm. But her lost father (Michael Melia) arrives to cheer her up. Rob and Max kiss for Christmas and Duffy invites Charlie to share her turkey. Even Ash and Nikki make up.

EPISODE 16 THE TIES THAT BIND
by Stephen Wyatt

Nikki tells Ash she is pregnant. A divorced father kidnaps his young daughter who is violently sick. He takes her to casualty where gastroenteritis is suspected. He lies about the mother's whereabouts and Duffy is suspicious. The mother (Shirin Taylor) arrives, threatening a restraining order. A young woman executive (Amanda Redman) with a broken wrist comes in with her assistant, who turns out to be her lover, much to her husband's horror. Sandra is upset about Julian and Duffy is alarmed that the locum consultant is her son's father, Andrew. A wedding is wrecked when the bridegroom and best man, who also loves the girl, fight drunkenly on a beach after the stag party. The concussed bridegroom is rushed into casualty and recovers.

EPISODE 17 LIFE IN THE FAST LANE
by Susan Wilkins

A drunk driver (Hywel Bennett) jumps a set of traffic lights and hits two men and a woman. One man is pinned under his car and Andrew, called to the scene, certifies that he is dead. The other man needs a chest drain and the woman has a broken leg. The driver runs away, reappearing after the ambulance arrives, claiming he was also hit and lying that the driver fled and was black. In casualty the police discover the truth. A depressed teenager is brought in by her mother (Heather Tobias). She admits to having taken an overdose of paracetamol days earlier. Andrew tells her parents that her condition will deteriorate and she is likely to die. Ash and Nikki talk about abortion.

EPISODE 18 EVERYBODY NEEDS SOMEBODY
by Arthur McKenzie

A mentally ill man (Stephen Moore) takes pills, cuts his wrists and tries to gas himself, to the horror of his barrister sister (Angela Pleasance). When the paramedics arrive, the man tries to strangle Josh and knife Jane. Josh is treated in casualty. His wife visits, treating Jane jealously. Nikki phones Ash to tell him she has had an abortion. An old farmer taunts his nephew before suffering a tractor accident. Both legs are severed. Rob and Sandra rush out to tend him but he dies in crash. Duffy's son Peter arrives at the end of her shift. Andrew meets him for the first time.

EPISODE 19 GETTING INVOLVED
by Sam Snape

Dr Mike Barratt, the new consultant, is welcomed to the department and treats a young depressed mother who has slashed her breasts, baffling her husband. A busy couple (Michael Cashman and Paula Wilcox) who run a sandwich bar leave their young son to fix his own snack at home. He electrocutes himself on a powerpoint and is rushed into casualty and then intensive care as his agonized parents blame each other. Unhappy Max tells Charlie her dad has left home. An elderly woman, bullied by her friend and rival in love for sixty years, is both sad and relieved when her friend has a stroke and dies in casualty. Duffy cooks Andrew dinner.

EPISODE 20 DIVIDED LOYALTIES
by Robin Mukherjee

In the 100th episode Ash learns he has won promotion to Senior Staff Nurse. A truant is knocked down as he runs from his schoolmaster. The man has been bullying him and continues to do so in casualty. A desperate unemployed young father joins a ram-raiding gang. They plan to

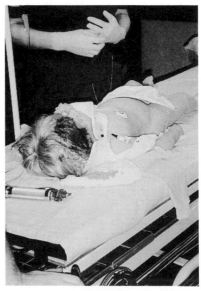

A baby is fatally injured by ram raiders. Luckily she's made of jelly

raid the electrical shop where his wife works. The van ploughs through the shop window, into his wife and their baby daughter who dies in crash. Max's father visits and reveals he is infatuated by a young woman. Norma asks a tetchy Charlie to be allowed to go home because her mother has died. Max arranges an after-shift drink to congratulate Ash. Charlie doesn't attend.

EPISODE 21 — FAMILY MATTERS
by Robin Mukherjee

Norma is in mourning. Two tramps are mugged by a gang of youths and one later dies in crash from his wounds. One of the gang has a gashed arm and turns up in casualty. He is forced to admit the attack. A smart young couple come in. The girl is faking pains. They leave, having stolen drugs and equipment for the thrill of it. A young girl who's vomiting blood is brought in by her sister and teenage brother who were babysitting. Mike realises she has been sexually abused. They conclude that the abuser must be the father, to the horror of his wife (Elizabeth Estensen). It transpires that the brother is the guilty one – but he too may have been abused.

EPISODE 22 — CHILD'S PLAY
by Jacqueline Holborough

Charlie agrees reluctantly to see a pyschiatrist who diagnoses depression. A rent boy is picked up in a bar by a middle class man who takes him to a flat. There he's gang-raped, beaten and later dumped in a road. The lad does not explain but Rob soon discovers the rectal injuries and surgery is needed. Max has an uneasy meeting with her dad's girlfriend. A boarding school pupil, who is having an affair with a much fancied teacher, is 'bumped' by her schoolmates. Her back is broken. In casualty Mike fears she will be paralysed and lambasts the teacher, who has also made her pregnant. A manic father who hates taking anti-depressants is brought in by his son. Unshaven and dazed, Charlie argues with Duffy then collapses in his office from stress.

EPISODE 23 — NO CAUSE FOR CONCERN
by Bryan Elsley

Charlie spends a night on the settee and turns up for work although Duffy urges him to take the day off. Rob has landed a General Surgery job in Southampton. In a docked cargo ship, hired hands are overcome with fumes when they misunderstand instructions. One, a young Chinese, dies. The overworked First Officer goes to help and is injured. With him in casualty, the ship's captain (Julian Holloway) has to admit he pushed them too far. Two young boys steal a security van not realising it is carrying radioactive isotopes. When they crash, the isotopes are scattered. With Josh and Jane unwittingly contaminated, and forced to strip and shower in casualty, a bossy nuclear specialist insists the unit be hosed down and closed down. Sandra is angry. No one will come clean about the risks.

EPISODE 24 — BOILING POINT
by Peter Bowker

Duffy has news: she's marrying Andrew the next day. Sandra is planning a second honeymoon with her husband David. Simon gives Rob an engraved Filofax. Max is to train as a nurse. On a housing estate an old man is brutally beaten and robbed in his son's home. The son (Michael Angelis) gets his neighbours, part of a vigilante group, to tour the estate with baseball bats. By now the youths are ready to fight and battle begins. The father of one of the youths is knifed by the leader. The ambulances go in although the police are not to be seen. Some youths follow the ambulance as it brings the victims to casualty. They break into the basement and start a fire. Max sounds the alarm and waiting patients are pushed out as an ambulance is petrol-bombed by the jubilant youths. It blasts the reception and crash where Mike and Rob are attempting emergency surgery. They stagger into the grounds but Rob lingers to remove one of the victims. A second explosion brings the roof down on top of him. As firemen fight the blaze, Duffy believes it is the end of the Holby A & E department.

Geraint Morris, the daddy of *Casualty*, had said his farewells. He was off to Lima to talk to drug dealers and customs officers and community workers as he had once talked to nurses and doctors and ambulance men. He hoped his new drama, *White Princess of Death*, would go into production in 1993.

Michael Ferguson, former producer of *EastEnders*, expected to spend 1993 working on a lavish adaptation of the Hornblower books for BBC Television. Alas, it proved too costly and the order came to set the project aside. Gloom descended. Then the telephone rang. It was Peter Cregeen, Head of Drama Series, with an oh-so-casual suggestion about *Casualty*. Michael said equally casually that he'd mull over the idea. Five minutes later he had rung his boss back. The answer was: 'Yes please, yes.'

'It's a marvellous series. Any producer would give his right arm to be connected with it,' he says. 'I shan't be making any glaringly obvious changes. Slight changes in emphasis, perhaps. I like exciting stories in the framework of a modern morality play. At the moment we don't know if *Casualty* will become a twice-weekly series. We have no crystal ball. So we're concentrating on fifty-minute episodes. It is possible to offer hard-hitting drama for the early evening, we proved that with *EastEnders*.'

The 1992 double-length series had been a success, both in terms of record high audiences and their appreciation of what they watched, borne out by the research. Every episode scored over eighty per cent on the scale of enjoyable entertainment. It was not surprising, then, that twenty-four episodes of Holby life were commissioned for 1993.

New boy Michael set about hiring the new

Opposite: A spectacular train crash tests the Holby team in the first episode

THE TROLLEYS ROLL FOR 1993

Those rioting youths may have set fire to Holby's Accident and Emergency ward but what actually burned was a duplicate set made in another part of the warehouse. That's why a speedily 're-built' department is back in business so soon.

Michael Ferguson is the new producer

Holby staff. He decided that it was again time to employ a woman junior doctor. Enter Karen Goodliffe, working class, chip on shoulder, sometimes blunt to the point of rudeness but a damn fine doctor. Big Mike Barratt, the consultant, will need all his patience and charm with her. To fill the gap left by Staff Nurse Sandra, enter sensible cheerful Adele Beckford, Jamaican origins, motherly in the warm but unsentimental way that Megan Roach was motherly.

Also joining the nursing team is Ken Hodges, a bright, good-looking former medical student. He happens to be gay. So what? So nothing unless you're talking to the new porter, Frankie Drummer, a former factory hand, salt of the earth, admirer of Page Three girls and quick with the 'poofter' cracks. He likes his new job and is soon able to diagnose the patients' problems and give advice quicker than the doctors. Or so he thinks.

We're still in a recession and Holby Hospital Trust is still counting its pounds. Slimy Simon Eastman, the administrator in 1992, has suffered a sharp shove sideways. In his place comes Surgical Manager Mark Calder, slim, suave and straight out of industry. He won't be dictated to by these head-in-the-clouds medical people. They must accept they're part of a business now. He's not happy that they've hired two new nurses. Nor is he pleased that the department still employs Norma Sullivan as a receptionist. So it's his idea to bring pretty Japanese Mie Nishi-Kawa across from another office to work alongside the tetchy old bat. She'll get the message. Or at least, that's the plan.

And how will 1993 treat our old friends? Josh opts for yet more specialized training. Jane makes a bold decision to switch direction. Duffy is now Mrs Andrew Bower, mother of one. She's settled at last but her biological clock is ticking fast, or so she believes. Charlie has recovered.

Top: Mark Calder (Oliver Parker) is the new holder of the Holby purse strings
Above: Mike Barratt tries not to look down on his new SHO Karen Goodliffe
Opposite: Staff Nurse Adele Beckman (Doña Kroll) has to keep keen student nurse Helen Chatsworth (Samantha Edmonds) in check